HEINEMANN
Integrated Skills
intermediate

BRUCE MILNE

SERIES EDITOR PHILIP PROWSE

Heinemann International
A division of Heinemann Educational Books Ltd
Halley Court, Jordan Hill, Oxford OX2 8EJ

OXFORD LONDON EDINBURGH
MADRID ATHENS BOLOGNA PARIS
MELBOURNE SYDNEY AUCKLAND SINGAPORE TOKYO
IBADAN NAIROBI HARARE GABORONE
PORTSMOUTH (NH)

ISBN 0435 28239 5

First published 1991

Cover by Carrie Craig

Acknowledgements

While every effort has been made to trace the owners of the copyright material in this book, there have been some cases where the publishers have been unable to find sources or contact the owners. We should be grateful to hear from anyone who recognises their copyright material and who is unacknowledged. We shall be pleased to make the necessary corrections in future editions of the book.

The author and publisher would like to thank the following for their kind permission to use their material in this book.
Dateline, advertisement and photograph p.26; Emap Metro, **Work Matters**, p15; Friends of the Earth, publicity leaflet p.53; Celia Ann Glover, **Views of a Park** p.27; Heinemann Educational Books, **Reading About Biology** (extract) by Stewart Kellington and Wilf Stout p.51; HMSO card is reproduced with the permission of the Controller of Her Majesty's Stationery Office, p.12; Kim Hull, Adventure Balloons leaflet p.23; *Just 17*, extracts by Annabel Goldstorb pp2 and 3; Simon and Schuster Young Books, **Antarctic Survival** (extracts) by Robert Shaw p.33; Solo Agency, **Toshaiki Yasuda** p.6; extract reproduced from **Improve Your Running Skills** by kind permission of Usborne Publishing Ltd, London, p.47; extracts from **The Directory of Summer Jobs Abroad** published by Vacation Work p.16; Chris Winn, cartoons taken from **The Friends of the Earth Handbook**, published by Macdonald Optima at £5.99, pp.52 and 53.

Photographs

Associated Press, p.35; Barnaby's Picture Library, p.56; Michael Boyd, p.29; Oxford Scientific Films, p.50; Greg Evans Photo Library, pp.7 and 28 (A and B); The Hutchison Library, p.48; ICCE Photo Library, p.54; Bruce Milne, pp.28 (D) and 43; John Redman, p.55; Virgin Atlantic Airways Ltd, p.15

Illustrated by

Nancy Anderson pp.13, 31, 34, 42
Barbara Crow pp.14, 20, 30
Anthony Sidwell pp.32, 36
Paul Slater pp.2, 3, 8, 9, 10, 11, 24, 46
Tony Wilkins (Oxford Illustrators) pp.22, 40, 41, 47
Willow pp.5, 16, 37, 38, 39, 58, 59, 60, 61

Designed by

Learning Materials Design, Newport Pagnell, Bucks.
(Bo Elderton, Shirley Scripps, David Wolfson)

Typeset by

Learning Materials Design, Newport Pagnell, Bucks.

Printed and bound in Great Britain by

Thomson Litho Ltd., East Kilbride, Scotland

91 92 93 94 95 10 9 8 7 6 5 4 3 2

Contents

Map of the book

	TOPIC	SKILLS

	TOPIC	**SKILLS**

UNIT 4 HOLIDAYS

LESSON

	TOPIC	SKILLS

UNIT 8 SPORT

UNIT 9 THE NATURAL WORLD

UNIT 10 TIME

Introduction

The aim of this book is to offer some genuinely integrated materials at intermediate level. The book is organised around ten units each containing three lessons covering one general theme. Although each lesson can be presented separately, it is recommended that all three lessons are taught to ensure that there is a balance of skills work covered. There is no particular order of units which the teacher should follow, but it should be pointed out that the later units are slightly more challenging in terms of lexis and content than the earlier units.

Authentic material has been selected which will interest the student. Reading material ranges from articles on Sumo wrestling to a psychological test to explain your character and listening material from teenagers talking about their parents' faults to a Vietnamese student describing his escape from Vietnam.

As well as practising the four skills: listening, speaking, reading and writing, there is plenty of opportunity for lexical development. There are several exercises designed to focus on and expand vocabulary areas and exercises to practise the skill of deducing the meaning of words from their context.

Most of the activities are task-based and lead towards a specific product. Usually this 'end product' is a piece of writing. The nature of the writing task is varied so that the students have to write letters and messages, design posters, write cartoon captions, prepare lists, write advertisements or leaflets, write a biography or even compose a poem. The texts help prepare the students for the end product by giving relevant information, providing a stimulus for discussion or presenting a suitable model for writing.

Also included in the book are Teacher's Notes which give suggestions as to how to exploit the material, a Key for the exercises in each lesson and a Tapescript.

 # Around the World

1   The popular magazine Just Seventeen asked its readers from around the world to send in details of their lives in different countries.

Below are articles about two of the readers. Complete the chart using information from the articles.

	Anke Kirschbaum	Blythe Gardner
Town		
School		
Entertainment	*Ballroom dancing*	
Rules and Regulations		*Must be home by 12.00*
Future Plans		

Anke Kirschbaum is 17 and lives in West Berlin, in the Federal Republic of Germany

◆ HOME:
"West Berlin is typical of any European city. I'm an only child and I live with my engineer father and my mother who works part-time in a tax consultant's office, in a terraced house very close to the wall."

◆ SCHOOL:
"In Germany we have several different types of secondary school. The Gymnasium (grammar school for the brightest pupils) where I attend the Realschule (for less bright), the Hauptschule (for the least bright) and the Gesamtschule (which is a comprehensive school for pupils of any ability)."

◆ ENTERTAINMENT:
"West Germany is quite expensive, especially compared with Britain. To earn extra pocket money I give private tuition in English three times a week, and earn about 200 marks (£70) a month, and I get 50 Marks (£17) a month from my parents.
"My main hobby is ballroom dancing and I have made a lot of friends through this. I also enjoy reading books (mostly in English), *Just Seventeen*, and writing letters.

I enjoy listening to Barbra Streisand, and my favourite actors are Fred Astaire and Katherine Hepburn.
"Every second Saturday I have school, but afterwards I meet friends and go out to the cinema or to a party. In West Berlin, we have the best nightlife in the whole of West Germany."

◆ RULES AND REGULATIONS:
"I have quite a good relationship with my parents and they let me do almost everything I choose. I have to be home by 10pm on weekdays and at the weekend they pick me up a little later. I am not very close with them, though. I prefer to confide in my friends.
"When I finish school, I would like to work in England, perhaps as a bilingual secretary for a year. But I'm not sure that I would like to live elsewhere permanently, for I greatly enjoy life in Berlin."

Blythe Gardner is 16 and lives in Lewistown, Montana, USA

◆ HOME:
"Most people in our town are retired. The main source of income is agriculture and the area is pretty and mountainous with lots of wide open spaces.

"My parents are divorced, and I live with my mother who works as a doctor's receptionist. My father raises cattle and farms on a ranch just outside of the town."

◆ SCHOOL:
"I go to a mixed-sex high school with about 700 pupils. At the end of our senior year we get a diploma. Then I plan to go to university. I also own a small herd of cows, and each fall I sell the old ones and buy a new batch. I put the profit in the bank and use it as I need it."

◆ ENTERTAINMENT:
"I don't go out much during the week because there's nothing to do in this small town. Usually I watch TV or read books. On Friday and Saturday nights, there is usually a school sporting event (basketball or football) and after the game, everybody gets in their cars (I got my licence when I was 15) with their friends and 'cruise'. This means you drive up and down Main Street and if you see someone you know or would like to know – you flash your headlights and pull them over to talk."

◆ RULES AND REGULATIONS:
"We are not allowed in to bars until we are 21, so if there is no game, we usually go to a drive-in movie. I have to be home by 12am.

"I think people in the US miss out on the exposure to different countries and cultures that you enjoy in Europe. We also miss out on the social pub scene, but I like the fact that America has so many interesting facets."

2 Which of the two girls do you think has a better life?
Where would you prefer to live – West Berlin or Lewistown? Why?

3 **a** Find a word or expression in the article about Anke which means:

someone with no brothers or sisters
money that parents give to their children
entertainment at night such as films,
   theatre, discos, etc.
to tell your secrets to
able to speak two languages fluently

b Find a word in the article about Blythe which means:

no longer working
no longer married
someone who answers the phone and
   receives guests
money you earn from a business
the piece of paper which shows you have
   passed your driving test

4 Interview another student about their hobbies and interests and their school and home life. As you interview them, make notes on the information using the following headings.

Home
School
Entertainment
Rules and Regulations
Future Plans

H OMEWORK

Write an article for the magazine *Just Seventeen* either about yourself or about the student you interviewed. Use the headings in **4**.

2 Living at Home

1 *'I have to be home by 10 pm on weekdays'*, says Anke Kirschbaum. Were/are your parents strict or lenient? What rules did/do your parents insist on? Answer these questions for yourself and then ask another student.

	Self	Friends
Were/are you allowed to smoke in the house?		
Were/are you allowed to drink alcohol?		
Could/can you have any friends you wanted/want?		
Could/can you wear the clothes you wanted/want?		
Were/are you allowed to have parties in the house?		
Did/do you have to keep the house tidy?		
Were/are you allowed to keep pets?		
What time did/do you have to come home by?		
Did/do your parents make you do your homework?		
How much pocket money did/do your parents give you?		

Who had/has the stricter parents?

2 Steph and Rudi talk about their parents.

 a Listen to Steph and decide which of the following she talks about.

her parents' age
the housework
being punished
pocket money
wearing make-up
her brother
smoking and drinking
borrowing the car
her parents' love

 b Listen to Rudi and answer these questions.

(i) What two rules does she mention?
(ii) How was she punished when she did something wrong?
(iii) What did she have to do in exchange for her pocket money?
(iv) What problem did her parents have?

3 Read the sentences below. Do you agree with them? Mark them like this:

1 I completely agree with the statement.
2 I partly agree. It depends on the situation.
3 I'm not sure.
4 I disagree.

- Children should be allowed to wear what they want.

- The best way to punish children is to stop them from going out in the evening or at the weekend.

- Either the father or the mother should stay at home until the children go to school.

- You should make sure your children go to bed at a regular time. You shouldn't let them stay up later than this.

- Children should be allowed to smoke and drink if they want to.

- You should make sure that your children come home at a fixed time – before 11.00 if they are under 16. Children need to have rules.

- Parents tend to give more freedom to boys than girls. This is wrong. Boys and girls should be treated the same.

- It is better for everybody if children leave home when they are 18.

Now compare your answers with some other students. Do you have the same ideas? If not, try to explain your ideas.

4 *How to be a good parent.* Discuss with some other students what advice you would give to parents on how to bring up their children.

HOMEWORK

How to be a good parent. Following your discussion, write your own set of rules to parents which gives advice about the best way to bring up children.

3 Another Country

1 a Many people live in a different country from the one they were born and grew up in. Why does this happen? Make a list of reasons.

b Which of the countries below would you prefer to live in? Why? Make a list of your reasons and explain why to another student.

United States of America
Italy
Japan
Soviet Union
Australia
Thailand

2 What are the difficulties you would face when you first arrived in another country? Add five more difficulties to the one given below.

• learning a new language

Discuss your list with another student.

3 Read the article about Toshiaki Yasuda and answer the following questions.

a Why did he come to Britain?
b List five things he likes about Britain.
c What does he miss about his own country?

TOSHIAKI YASUDA is public relations manager for the Nissan Motor Co, whose £65 million plant at Washington, Tyne and Wear, is now producing 140 Nissan Bluebirds a day. He moved from Tokyo to England three years ago, and lives in East Sheen, near Richmond with his wife Yoshiko, his son Hidetomo, 17, (who now calls himself Tom), and his daughter Akiko, 14. He works an 11-hour day and visits the Washington plant about once a week.

'When we arrived it was winter – no sunshine, day in day out. Quite a lot of Japanese wives get depressed about it when they first come here. But springtime is fantastic. You have beautiful gardens, and I was amazed at the really big parks. I've become a little bit English in that I've started gardening, trimming plants and cutting the grass. I've also started growing roses with help from my neighbour.

'We have about 20 Japanese at the factory in Washington. They're impressed by the friendliness of the people. If I've been working at Sunderland on a Friday I quite often stay on and play golf with my colleagues on Saturday. A lot of Japanese people take up golf here – it's about a tenth of the cost compared with Japan.

'Coming here has meant a great change of lifestyle. I think the quality of life is better here. In Japan, the cost of property is horrendous. We had a flat in Tokyo – our house here is 50 per cent bigger. We're only five minutes' walk from Richmond Park, and I will miss the theatres, concerts and musicals when I go home. British food is not as bad as some people say; I like roast beef.

'I'm more conscious of my family here, and I feel a greater need to spend time with them. My daughter has become very Anglicised in her speech and behaviour. I think that's a good thing. The only thing I miss about Japan is the mountains as my hobby is climbing.'

4 Theresa is a foreigner living in Britain. She speaks about life in Britain. Make notes on what she likes and doesn't like about it.

Likes	Dislikes
Cambridge	*Bad weather*

5 Listen to Theresa again and answer the following questions.

a Why did she come to Britain?
b When did she first come to Britain?
c What does she miss about her own country?

H OMEWORK

What do you think it is like for a foreigner to live in your country? What are the advantages and disadvantages? Imagine you are a foreigner. Write a letter to a friend back in England giving your impressions of the country.

4 Missing People

Did you know that approximately 25 000 people go missing in Britain every year?

1 When someone rings up the police station to report a missing person, what questions do you think a policeman would ask? Add questions to the one below.

- When did you last see your husband?

2 Label the picture using the words below.

beard	jacket
cheeks	lips
eyebrows	moustache
forehead	neck
glasses	shirt
hair	tie

3 Listen to a woman who is reporting someone missing and complete the form below.

REPORT OF MISSING PERSON

Name _____

Age _____

Sex _____

Marital Status _____

Address _____

_____

Telephone _____

Physical Features _____

_____

_____

Last seen: Time _____

             Place _____

             Clothes _____

Additional Information _____

_____

_____

Form M/73

---

4 Listen again and decide which of the following is the missing person.

5 Look at this poster. Which of the men in **4** does it describe?

A

B

C

D

E

F

HAVE YOU SEEN THIS MAN?

The police urgently need to speak to this man. His name is Ronald Dodds and he is thought to be residing in the Bath area. He is 6 ft 2 ins. tall and has got short dark hair, a moustache and brown eyes. He usually wears glasses. He was last seen wearing a brown suit and a dark green overcoat. If you see anybody resembling this description, do not approach him but call the police on this number: (0856) 236

A reward of £200 will be paid for information which leads to his arrest.

HOMEWORK

Choose someone in your group and make a poster describing them in the same way as in **5**.

9

5 Accident

1 Would you make a good witness? Look at the picture below for two minutes. How much can you remember?

2 What do these words mean? Discuss them with another student. Use the accident report opposite to help you.

seat belt	swerve
crash into	brake
pedestrian	windscreen
crossroads	damage
ambulance	pavement
injured	bodywork

Statement

I was driving along West Road at a reasonable speed when, about fifty metres before the crossroads, a pedestrian walking on the pavement suddenly ran across the road in front of me. I braked as hard as I could, but I had to swerve to avoid the pedestrian. I crashed into a car which was parked by the side of the road. Fortunately, the pedestrian wasn't injured, but I had a bad cut on my face caused when my head hit the windscreen. I had forgotten to put on my seat belt. An ambulance took me to hospital where I had to have five stitches. There was a lot of damage to my car; the windscreen was broken and the bodywork was badly dented. I was interviewed by the police in hospital.

3 Have you ever seen or had an accident? Work with some other students and ask each other about accidents you have seen or had.

4 How do you think the government of your country could reduce the number of car accidents? Make a list of proposals under these headings.

Driving Test
Roads and speed limits
Seat belts
Drinking and driving
Young people and old people

5 You were the witness of a car accident. Using the information in the form below, write an account of the accident stating clearly what you saw. Begin: *On the 18th February at 2.30 pm, I was standing on the corner of …*

Form M 465

DETAILS OF TRAFFIC ACCIDENT

Date	18 February
Time	2.30 pm
Place	High Street, Banbury, Oxfordshire
Weather	Dry, clear visibility
Vehicles involved	Blue Volkswagen E 385 TYJ Grey Ford Escort B 937 JOK
Injuries	None

Sketch Map of Accident

HIGH STREET

WITNESS X

LONG ROAD

A — BLUE VOLKSWAGEN
B — GREY FORD ESCORT

6 Burglary

1 What do burglars usually steal from houses? Work with another student and make a list of items.

2 Has anybody in your group ever had anything stolen? Find out what was stolen and when and where it happened.

3 What precautions should you take if you leave your house for two or three weeks to go on holiday? Work with another student and make a list of things you should do.

4 Read the card below.

Keep this card

Don't let them get away with it

Dial 999

Help the police

What to do if you see or hear anything suspicious

You can help to reduce crime

Your police force needs your help in beating the criminal. They can't do their job without it. You can help best by reporting at once anything that strikes you as suspicious.

If you saw someone being attacked or robbing a shop, you would naturally phone the police. But ring them just the same if you see someone lurking around your neighbour's side door or trying car doors. The police would prefer a false alarm to a burglary or a stolen car. And ring at once – seconds count.

What you should do

Dial 999. Ask for Police and tell them as much as you can:
1 Where the incident happened
2 The number of people involved
3 Description of the suspects
4 Description of the scene
5 Registration number of any vehicles involved
6 Your name and address will help, but they are not essential

5 Kate Wilkinson works at the switchboard of a busy London police station. Listen to the call she gets and, as you listen, note down which of the facts numbered 1–6 in the card in **4** are given.

6 When the Greens came back from their holiday they found that they had been burgled. Listen to Mr Green describing to a police officer what has been stolen from his house. As you listen, decide which of the following articles are being described.

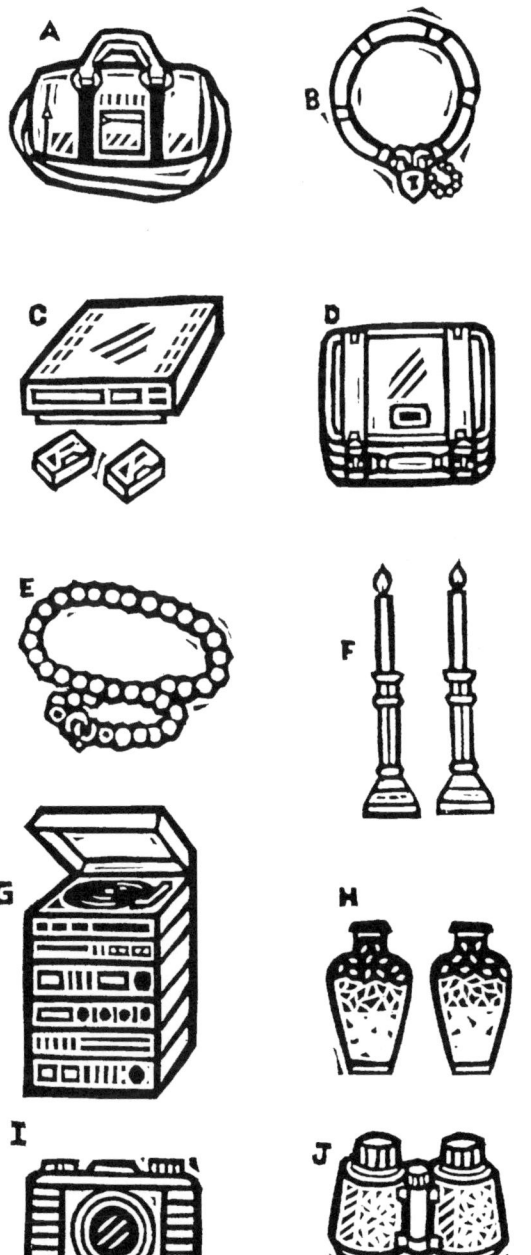

7 Listen again to Mr Green and complete the list of stolen items giving as much detail as possible.

Stolen Items

1　*Ferguson video*

2

3

4

5

6

7

H OMEWORK

Write a set of instructions for people leaving their houses to go on holiday. Add to the list below.

Checklist
Lock all doors and windows

13

7 Which Job?

1 Look at the list of jobs below and choose the one that you would most like to do and the one that you would least like to do.

nurse
journalist
shop assistant
manager of a football team
policeman/woman
air steward/stewardess
cook
car mechanic
disc jockey
farmer

Compare your choices with another student and explain your reasons.

2 Which of the following qualities do you think are important in an air steward/stewardess?

good looks
intelligence
knowing several languages
good eyesight
physical fitness
a technical knowledge of aeroplanes
smart clothes
the ability to swim
patience
knowing how to look after babies
a knowledge of First Aid

3 Listen to Mark's conversation with the recruitment officer at Virgin Atlantic, an airline which carries passengers from London to America. What are the job requirements? Fill in the chart below.

Age

Height

Other requirements

4 Read the article opposite in which an air stewardess talks about her work. Match the titles below with the right paragraph.

Training
The Route and my Job
Getting the Job
Working Hours
Introducing Debbie Mason
Social Life and Family Life
Health Problems

WORK MATTERS

There's more to being an air hostess than serving packaged meals to overweight businessmen.

✳ ✳ ✳

Debbie Mason, 24, has risen through the ranks to become an in-flight purser (head stewardess) with Virgin Atlantic. She told Sue Wheeler about her life on Richard Branson's airline and what it takes to get on in this high-flying job.

✳ ✳ ✳

Some time ago I was working in an office when I saw a picture of Richard Branson and read about him starting a new airline, Virgin. I sent him a letter saying I was interested in working for him. After a successful interview with a recruitment officer, I began their four-week training course. The personnel officers say it's usually obvious at the start whether somebody has the right qualities or not. Personality is very important. You have to be flexible, attractive, very well-groomed and able to smile when duty calls – even if you don't feel like it. Obviously you don't need airline experience, but nursing, or other work with people, is useful.

✳ ✳ ✳

The training course is really common sense although the practical side includes things like life-boat sessions in a swimming pool, fire fighting in a smoke-filled room and learning how to deliver a baby. In reality, though, you end up dealing mainly with travel sickness. The point is you have to be prepared for everything.

I had to pass exams in safety equipment procedures and first-aid which are required by the Civil Aviation Authority (CAA), plus Virgin's own cabin services course.

✳ ✳ ✳

I work on flights from Gatwick to New York or Miami. And I'm definitely not a glorified waitress! Only 10% of my work involves serving people. The emphasis is on safety and that's what we're here for. Before every flight there's a briefing where the crew are asked questions on first-aid and safety.

✳ ✳ ✳

I think this job ages you. On flights to New York I'm on board from 2.15 in the afternoon until nearly midnight our time. I'm supposed to drink eight pints of water per flight to prevent my body from dehydrating, but it's nearly impossible to get through that much. So my skin is probably suffering. But I think these are minor disadvantages. When we go to New York it's only 6.55 pm American time and we usually go out and have a party!

✳ ✳ ✳

I fly about four or five times in a 28 day roster, which means I work hard for two or three days, then take time off. I get at least eight days off every month, so it doesn't feel like most other full-time jobs. I get four weeks holiday a year, three of which have to be in the winter. But as one of my perks is being able to fly with any airline for 10% of the normal cost, I can afford to go to far away places in search of winter sun.

✳ ✳ ✳

It's a sociable job on board and off. There are only 220 crew members in total so we do know each other pretty well. This means things are very friendly and I think it's obvious to the passengers that we're having a good time, which helps them relax. When people leave Virgin to work for other airlines they often miss the intimacy of a small company and come back. But although the social life with Virgin is fabulous, outside it's non-existent. Friends and family know my time off is precious, but even at home I'm sometimes on standby. The job puts a strain on any romance. Happily my boyfriend works for Virgin too, and we chose to work a 'married roster' which means we fly together all the time. It's either this or take a chance you'll bump into each other once in a while.

5 Decide whether the following statements are true or false. If they are false, correct them.

    a   She enjoys working for Virgin Atlantic.
    b   Serving food takes up most of her time.
    c   Virgin Atlantic recommends that she drinks a lot of water during flights.
    d   She has less free time than people do in most other jobs.
    e   She can get cheap flights on any airline.
    f   She doesn't see her boyfriend very often.

HOMEWORK

Choose the job that you would most like to do. Write a paragraph describing the requirements for the job and what the job involves.

8 Applying for a Job

1 Would you like the opportunity to work in another country? Read the advertisements below and answer the following questions.

Which job:

a requires you to be over 18?
b only lasts for a maximum of two and a half weeks?
c requires you to work for a minimum of six weeks?
d offers you a place where you can cook?
e requires you to know a foreign language?
f gives you two days off per week?
g asks you to work twelve hours a day?
h doesn't pay you any money?

1 HOTEL CANNERO: 28051 Cannero Riviera, Italy, (Tel: 323 788046).

WAITERS/WAITRESSES (2), SWIMMING POOL/TENNIS COURT ATTENDANTS, BAR STAFF, KITCHEN STAFF. Around £33 per week. 12 hours per day, 6 days per week. Free board and accommodation. Knowledge of German, Italian or French required. Period of work 3 or 6 months between end of March and end of October. Applications from 25th March to Maria Carla Gallinotto at the above address.

2 C.O.C. GMBH: Bayerstrasse 57, 8000 Munchen 2, Germany (Tel: 089 5306643).

CHAMBERMAIDS (30): required for various hotels in Munich. To work 8 hours per day, 5 days per week. Wage of £530 per month, approximately. Board and accommodation not provided. Minimum period of work 6 weeks. No knowledge of languages required. Applicants should be healthy, organised and clean. Applications to the above address as soon as possible.

3 VACATION WORK INTERNATIONAL: 9 Park End Street, Oxford OX1 IHJ.

GRAPE PICKERS required in the South of France from mid-September for 2 to 2½ weeks. Applicants should be over 16 years. Self-catering accommodation provided plus about £20 per day.
For full details write to Vacation Work International enclosing a stamped addressed envelope.

4 CHANTIERS JEUNESSE MAROC: B.P. 1351 Rabat, 31 Rue du Liban, Morocco.

Organises international work camps throughout Morocco to help with regional development projects. Construction of schools and youth centres, social welfare work. Work is unpaid and there is a registration fee of about £4. Free board and accommodation is provided. Camps last about 3 weeks and an 8 hour day is normally worked. Volunteers must be at least 18 years of age. All applications should be sent to the address shown above.

2 Judith and Sharon are discussing the advertisements. They want to do a holiday job together. Listen to their conversation and answer the questions below.

a Which job does Sharon mention first?
b Which job does Sharon mention next?
c Which job does Judith want to do?
d Which one do they finally choose?

3 Now listen to them again and answer the following questions .

a Why doesn't Judith want to take the job in Morocco?

b Why is Sharon worried about going to Germany?

c Why doesn't Judith want to take the job in Italy?

---

a

b

c

d

We would like to apply for the job of chambermaid as advertised in the handbook 'Holiday Jobs Abroad'. We are school leavers and are looking for summer employment before going on to further education in October. We feel sure that the experience of visiting another country would be very stimulating and enjoyable. It would also have the advantage of allowing us to improve our knowledge of German. We are both 18 years old and fit and healthy. We are available for work from June 20th to the end of September and we would like to work for a period of six weeks if possible. References can be obtained from:

        Mr G Hobbit
        Headmaster
        Greenway 6th Form College
        Long Road
        Cambridge
        CB1 6TH

We would be grateful if you could let us know if you can employ us as soon as possible.

e

f

---

4 Read the letter Judith wrote.

Where should the following information be positioned on the letter?

(i)   C.O.C. GMBH
         Bayerstrasse 57
         8000 Munchen 2
         Germany

(ii)   Yours faithfully

(iii)   Dear Sirs

(iv)   Thursday 16th March

(v)   *Judith West*
          Sharon Beck

(vi)   248 Metcalfe Street
          Cambridge
          CB1 4DG

HOMEWORK

Choose one of the jobs. Write a letter of application.

9 The Interview

1 When you apply for a job, you often have to go for an interview. What is the best way to get the job? Discuss the following statements with another student. Which of the statements in each pair do you think gives the best advice?

1 a You should always wear your best clothes when you go for an interview.

b Employers nowadays don't mind what you wear as long as you don't look like a punk.

2 a You should never smoke during an interview.

b It's all right to smoke, provided that you ask for permission first.

3 a There's nothing you can do to stop being nervous – it's quite normal.

b If you appear nervous in front of the interviewers, they are more likely to give the job to someone else.

4 a It's a good idea to agree with the interviewer.

b If you disagree with the interviewer, he/she will be impressed that you have got your own ideas.

5 a You should find out as much about the job as possible before you go.

b You will be told about the job when you go for the interview.

2 Read the advice below on interviews. Do you agree with the advice?

Everybody is nervous at interviews so don't worry about it. If it becomes a real problem, then go for a walk just before the interview and watch other people living their daily life – try to realise that if you fail the interview it is not the end of the world. There are other more important things in life. Try not to resort to having the drink before you go in – it's not a good idea to have the smell of alcohol on your breath!

It is obvious that you are expected to arrive on time, but a surprising number of people still manage to arrive late and this clearly makes a very bad impression, however good the excuse is. So make sure that you know exactly where you have to go and work out how you are going to arrive there with plenty of time to spare. If you do arrive early, you can always spend time looking around the premises. Decide if you would like to work there.

Even in this day and age it is still worth taking some trouble with your appearance, especially if you are going to an interview at a big multinational company or bank or insurance company. Put on your best clothes and make sure they are ironed. It is probably not a good idea to smoke during the interview – smoking has had such a bad press recently that it is not worth taking the risk. You may get someone who disapproves strongly!

Be polite but do not necessarily accept everything they say – be prepared to challenge some of their ideas. Employers are always happy to have people who have clear ideas and express their opinions with some force.

Do find out as much as you can about the company or institution before you go. Find out exactly what they do and find out as much as you can about the job you are applying for. If you can't find out certain things then make a note and ask them at the interview. Employers are always impressed when they find someone who has done their homework and someone with an enquiring mind – but plan your questions before you go. It is even worth writing them down on a piece of paper and looking at them again just before you go in. Finally, find out the name of the person who is going to interview you.

Try to predict what questions they might ask you. It's much easier to shine at an interview if you can answer questions quickly and efficiently.

Above all, show confidence. Tell them you are sure you can do the job and would enjoy the challenge and stimulation of working there.

3 Make a list of **do's** and **dont's** according to the advice in the article in **2**.

> **DO** arrive on time.
> **DON'T** smoke during the interview.

4 It is easier to do well in an interview if you have some idea of the questions they are going to ask you. Often it is possible to predict in advance what questions you will be asked.

Look at the job advertisement below. Make a list of questions that you think the applicant will be asked.

Bell College, Saffron Walden

requires

SOCIAL ACTIVITIES ASSISTANT

This residential college for overseas students requires a SOCIAL ACTIVITIES ASSISTANT to help with the college's varied social activities programme and to assist in the lively Student Services Office. Applicants should enjoy meeting students from all over the world. A friendly outgoing personality and an organised approach is essential and a knowledge of foreign languages would be helpful. This is a temporary appointment, initially for six months. Residential accommodation is available.

Applicants should send a C.V. to: The Principal's Secretary, Bell College, South Road, Saffron Walden, Essex CB11 3DP, Tel. (0799) 22918

---

5 Listen to interviews with two of the applicants for the job in **4** and fill in the details on the chart below.

	first applicant	second applicant
name	Beth Gordon	
age		
nationality	British	
previous experience		
additional information	Driving Licence	

6 Listen to the interviews again and decide which applicant you would give the job to and why.

10 Going Places

1 What do you need for a beach holiday in the sun? Write down as many things that you would need as you can think of in three minutes.

Compare your list with another student. Can you add any words to your list?

2 Listen to Melanie talking about holidays. Which of the following does she say are important for her when she goes on holiday?

good weather
sightseeing
nice shopping
exciting discos
cheap prices
interesting food
sports facilities
a beach to lie on

3 Listen again and find the answers to these questions.

a When was the holiday she talked about?
b How long did it last?
c Who did she go with?
d Why was Thailand an 'easy country to travel in'?
e How long did she spend in Australia?
f What sort of work did they get?
g What helped them to get jobs in Australia?

4 Think of one of the best holidays you have ever had. Make notes on the following:

When was it?
Where did you go?
Who did you go with?
How long did it last?
What did you do on holiday?
Why did you like it so much?

Work with another student. Interview each other about the best holidays you've ever had.

5 Match the picture with the activity.

archery   pottery   painting
camping   windsurfing   hang gliding
sailing   canoeing   wine tasting
horse riding   pot holing   climbing

6 Imagine you have won a competition and the prize is a holiday for four. Which of the following holidays would you personally choose?

A week's skiing holiday in the Swiss Alps – excitement and exhilaration in one of Switzerland's top resorts.

A ten day cruise in the Far East including stop-offs in Thailand, Singapore and Hong Kong – adventure and exoticism not to be missed. Also a chance to shop in the world's greatest shopping centres.

A fortnight on a Greek Island – sun, sea and gentle people; a relaxing holiday for those who want to get away from it all. A paradise for those who enjoy windsurfing and sailing.

Eight days on Safari in the game parks of Tanzania and Kenya – come and see the elephants, cheetahs and lions in their natural surroundings.

A gastronomic tour of French vineyards (this holiday will include extensive eating and wine-tasting). Instruction in painting and pottery available in the mornings.

An eight day multi-activity holiday in Scotland – with the opportunity to try some of the following: climbing, pot holing, canoeing, hang gliding, archery and horse riding.

A ten day visit to the Soviet Union, including guided tours of both Moscow and Leningrad – a fascinating look at one of the world's greatest countries.

Now work with some other students. You have to agree on one holiday that you would all like to go on. Discuss which one you would choose. Try to persuade the other students to agree to the holiday you have chosen.

H OMEWORK

Imagine you could go anywhere on holiday and do anything. Where would you go? What would you do? Plan your ideal holiday and write it as an advertisement.

11 Ballooning

1 Which of these sports have you tried?

parachuting   skiing
ballooning   deep-sea diving
rock climbing   motor racing

Which of them would you like to try? Put them in order of preference and explain your choice to another student.

2 Ballooning has become a popular sport in Britain. Like a lot of sports, ballooning has its own special language for the equipment and the parts of the balloon. Label the pictures using the words **in bold.**

The biggest part of a balloon is called the **envelope**. This is made of light nylon or polyester and varies in size from 566–3970 cubic metres. Near the top of the envelope is the **cooling vent**. This is a small hole which can be opened in flight to let some of the hot air escape and control the height of the balloon. At the bottom of the envelope is the **mouth**. This is where the hot air enters the envelope.

The passengers stand in the **basket**. This is usually rectangular in shape and made of rattan. In the middle of the basket is the **gas cylinder**. There

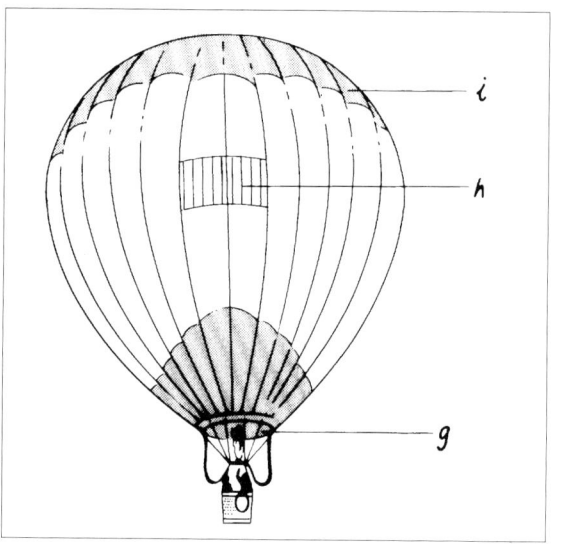

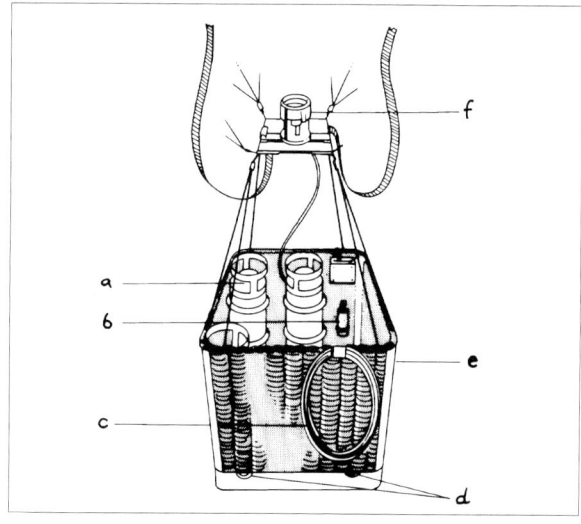

are usually some spare cylinders carried for use when the first one gets empty. Above the cylinder and just below the mouth of the envelope is the **burner** which is where the gas burns. As fire is a slight possibility, a **fire extinguisher** is also carried in the basket. Attached to the side of the basket is the **trailing rope**. This is only used at the end of a flight when a balloon lands. It helps to slow the balloon down. If you want to move the basket there are special **carrying handles** at the bottom of the basket.

3 *Adventure Balloons* is a company which offers weekend courses to people who would like to try ballooning. Read this extract from their brochure and answer the following questions.

a What is the best time of day to make a flight?
b What time do you have to get up?
c How many passengers can the balloon carry?
d How long does a typical flight last?
e How high does the balloon go?
f How can you get home at the end of a flight?

ADVENTURE BALLOONS

There are not many interests which mean leaving your bed at 5.30 am. But despite the drawback of boots and dew covered fields, Hot Air Ballooning has to be the most romantic way to fly. Few people can resist the attraction as three tons of nylon and hot air majestically rise with a roar from the propane burners.

'You don't feel as if you are moving at all. The ground just seems to drop away. And apart from the occasional thunder from the burners, there's just a great feeling of peace and tranquillity. When you break through the clouds, the balloon throws its shadows on them, multi-coloured, like a rainbow on their edges, and you feel you could walk on them, as if on a carpet.'

Flights are made early in the morning or evening because once the sun rises, conditions usually become too turbulent to permit take-off or landing.

The balloon travels at heights of up to 2 000 feet. When conditions permit, the flight will include some low-level flying, where you will be able to talk to interested spectators as you float slowly past.

Our balloons carry up to five people as well as one of our experienced and qualified pilots. Flight duration is about one hour, weather and daylight permitting. During the preparation for flight, you will be able to assist in the laying out and inflating of the envelope. Your flight direction and speed are wholly dependent on the prevailing wind. The balloon is tracked during its flight by the 'retrieve' car with which it is in radio contact. If wished, those 'in the basket' will be able to perform map reading and fly the balloon using its powerful burners at the discretion of the pilot. Alternatively, you may prefer to take photographs of the excellent views you get from the balloon basket.

People who have not done any ballooning before can relax in the knowledge that ballooning has the best safety record of all air sports.

HOMEWORK

Using your dictionary, make a list of the special equipment you need for a particular sport

12 Complaining

1 Have you, or anyone you know, ever complained about the following?

poor food in a restaurant
something you have bought in a shop which is no good
poor service on public transport
someone who hasn't done their job well (doctor, dentist, hairdresser, teacher, policeman, etc.)
bad service in a hotel

Who did you complain to? Did anything happen?

2 Read this advertisement for a weekend break.

Breakaway Tours

Flatford Country Club Lake District

▶ Two nights accommodation in luxurious centrally heated single room.

▶ TV and Snooker.

▶ Sports facilities include Olympic sized swimming pool, tennis courts, squash courts and fitness room.

▶ Breakfast (6.30 – 9.30) and Dinner (7.30 – 10.30) included.

▶ Minibus service from station.

▶ Excellent walking country – with possibility of local guides.

▶ Friendly family business.

▶ £125 all inclusive.

Write to *Flatford Country Club, Butterfield, Cumbria* or phone *0373 23519* for brochure and booking form.

3 Mrs Wallis went on the holiday at the Flatford Country Club but was not satisfied. Listen to her phone conversation with the travel agent who arranged it for her. Make a note of the things she complains about.

Compare your notes with another student.

4 Shortly after making the phone call, Mrs Wallis noticed this paragraph in her *Book of Weekend Breaks*.

' …should any of our recommendations fail to give complete satisfaction, we would be grateful if you would write to us giving an exact description of the cause or causes for complaint.

It is only by getting feedback from the customer that we can keep this guide up to date and accurate.'

Mrs Wallis decided to write a letter to the publishers of the book. Complete the letter she wrote using the notes you made from the phone call.

76 Bognor Road,
Brighton,
BN6 4WE

12th February

Dear Sirs

I am writing to complain about a holiday that I have recently had - which was one of those recommended in your guide book.

On the 2nd and 3rd of February of this year I spent two nights at the Flatford Country Club in the Lake District. Of course you cannot do anything about the awful weather - it was only to be expected in England in February. However, I was rather angry about the Country Club itself.

I arrived at Flatford station at 5.45 pm, but ....
....
Secondly, I would like to say something about my dog ....
....
In the advertisement for the holiday it mentions the tennis courts. However, I would like to point out that there is only one court and ....
....
You also mentioned local guides, but ....
....
I would have complained to the owners themselves, but it seemed that..
....

I am not someone who often complains, but I was disappointed with my holiday and for the price they are charging I think that they could provide a better service than they do. I would urge you to consider whether they should remain in your guide.

I thank you for your attention to this matter.

Yours sincerely

Amanda Wallis

13 Choosing Partners

1 In England more and more couples are finding marriage difficult. In fact, about one in every three marriages ends in divorce. But what makes a happy and successful couple? List five things you think are important for a happy marriage.

Now put your ideas in order of importance. Compare your list with some other students.

2 Read the advertisement below and find the answers to these questions.

a What is the name of the company being advertised?
b What is the service the company offers?
c What do you have to do to make use of this service?

What about you?

What do you think of this service?
Would you use the service yourself?
Do you think it would work for many people?

In 21 years *Dateline* introductions have been the start of many, many thousands of Love Stories …

If you would like a 'love story' of your own, a compatible partner to love and care for, and you are starting to wonder where you can find that special person, come to Dateline.

Many tens of thousands of people of all ages and occupations, from all over the country, join Dateline every year looking for someone to love. They want to meet someone with the same hopes, ambitions and aspirations as themselves, and are simply not meeting them socially or at work. Dateline, the largest, longest established, and most successful computer dating agency in the world, opens up a new circle of compatible people; people who could be living very close to you, but who, without Dateline, you might never meet.

'The world seemed made up of couples'

and Rita, wishing to find someone to share her social life, joined Dateline. Les realised that the right woman was not going to be easy to find, so thought Dateline was 'worth a try'. When he met Rita he 'fell in love straightaway.' Rita thought he was just what she needed with his easy ways, and it didn't take her long to realise that 'here was a very special man.' Marriage has not only given them the warm, loving homelife they wanted, but the place in society they felt they'd lost.

You *too* can find love

IF YOU ARE LOOKING FOR LOVE AND MARRIAGE, OR SIMPLY FRIENDS

Dateline has the widest selection of compatible people for you to meet, living as locally as you wish. Our reputation for a genuine, caring, and personal service is second to none, and Dateline's success speaks for itself in the many thousands of people who have found love and happiness through our service. Some of these true stories of people who were looking for someone special to share their lives, and were happily, amusingly, surprisingly matched by Dateline, are told in 'All you need is love' (a Sphere paperback £2.50)

If you would like to find out how Dateline's experience and care can work for you, simply complete the coupon below, and we will send you, totally free and without obligation, and of course in confidence, a full colour, comprehensive guide to exactly how Dateline works and also a FREE copy of 'All you need is love'.

Send today to: Dateline 23 Abingdon Road, London W8 6AH. Tel: 01 938 1011

---

3 Imagine it was your job to program the Dateline computer. Add the information you would need to this list.

- Name

- Age

Now discuss the following points with another student.

- Is it better to put together people who have the same interests or those who have different interests? What about character? Should they be the same or different?

- Should applicants be of the same age or doesn't it matter? What is the maximum age difference that you would allow?

- Would you put together people of different nationalities? Do you know of any examples of this? How has it worked?

- What about religion?

- What about height? What is the maximum difference that you would allow?

- Are there any other important considerations, i.e. smoking, love of pets, etc?

4 How many interests have you got in common with someone else? Work with another student and ask each other which of the activities on the Dateline coupon they are interested in.

FREE ⏵
START HERE ▼ **1**
I am over 17
Single ❏ Widowed ❏
Divorced ❏
Your sex __ (M/F)
Your height __ ft __ in
Age you would like to meet

- 'All you need is love' (a Sphere paperback) – stories of real people matching and meeting through Dateline
- A full colour guide to how Dateline can work for you
- Details of just one of the many Dateline members who could be your Perfect Partner

Occupation _____ Name_____
Religion _____ Address _____
Min ___ Max ___
_____

2 Tick ✓ which characteristics best describe you

3 Tick ✓ those activities you enjoy, put a ✗ against those you dislike and leave blank those where you have no preference

ARE YOU		DO YOU ENJOY			
Warmhearted	❏	Wine bars/Eating out	❏	Jazz/Folk music	❏
Serious	❏	Pubs	❏	Classical music	❏
Considerate	❏	Sports/Keep Fit	❏	Theatrical/Arts	❏
Shy	❏	Politics/History	❏	Watching TV	❏
Romantic	❏	Reading	❏	Smoking	❏
Fashion conscious	❏	Travelling	❏	Drinking	❏
Practical	❏	Science/Technology	❏	Being with children	❏
Conventional	❏	Cinema	❏	Homemaking	❏
Reliable	❏	Pets/Animals	❏	Gardening	❏
Adventurous	❏	Pop/Rock Music	❏	Countryside	❏

Dateline Dept (TMO), 23 Abingdon Road London W8 6AH Tel 01 338 1011

Have you got the same interests or are they different?
Which is the most popular activity in the group?
Which is the least popular activity in the group?
Are there any other activities you think should be included on the list?

H OMEWORK

Who is your ideal partner? Make a list of his/her qualities by completing the following sentences.

My ideal partner should be ...
My ideal partner should have ...

14 Judging People

1 There are many adjectives we use to describe someone's character. Can you match these words with the definitions opposite?

a warmhearted
b serious
c considerate
d shy
e romantic
f fashion conscious
g practical
h conventional
i reliable
j adventurous

Someone who:
(i) is interested in buying the latest clothes.
(ii) is frightened of meeting new people; wants to hide away.
(iii) likes to do things with their hands, such as mending a car or building a bookshelf.
(iv) likes to do things in a normal way, someone who doesn't like to be different.
(v) is kind and helpful to other people.
(vi) doesn't like to joke too much.
(vii) always does what they say they will do, someone you can trust and who will always be your friend.
(viii) is friendly, generous and likes to be with other people.
(ix) believes in love.
(x) is always wanting to try new things, even if they are dangerous.

2 Can you tell someone's character from his/her face? Look at the photographs and decide who is the most:

intelligent
conventional
serious
romantic
warmhearted

Which one would you most like to meet?
Which ones do you think you could be friends with?
Compare your opinions with another student.

A

B

C

D

3 Read these details about the people in the photographs in **2**. Can you guess which photographs they refer to?

CINTIA
Character
very talkative, sociable, enjoys meeting people

Hobbies and Interests
playing the piano, going to discos , watching TV, dogs, reading, Meryl Streep and Tom Cruise

---

JULIAN
Character
thoughtful, reasonably intelligent, sensitive, artistic, selfish

Hobbies and Interests
listening to all types of music, playing the drums, singing

MONICA
Character
can't make decisions, sensitive, easily hurt by what people say

Hobbies and Interests
classical music, ballet, going to parties

MICK
Character
reserved, generous

Hobbies and Interests
going to the cinema, travel, photography, writing novels

Try to decide on the age and nationality of each person.
Compare your opinions with another student.

4 Now listen to the people's voices. Does this help you to match them more accurately?

5 Look at the photographs below. Work with another student and invent a character for each of them. Include details about age, nationality, occupation, marital status, hobbies, interests and personal qualities. Compare your version with that of other students.

HOMEWORK

Write a description of one of these people.

---

15 Predicting Character

1 How can you tell someone's character? The following methods have all been used to analyse people's characters and predict their futures. Match them with the pictures below.

studying people's handwriting (graphology)
studying the position of the stars when people were born (astrology)
reading cards
studying the shape of people's bodies
analysing people's blood groups
reading palms

Which of these methods do you believe in?

2 Mrs Duvalier can predict the character and future of her clients.

a Listen to her talking to a client called Simon and decide which method she is using.

b Listen again. Which of the following does she say is true of him?

interested in ideas   relaxed
emotional   generous
serious   likeable
practical   warmhearted
kind

c List three things she says about his future.

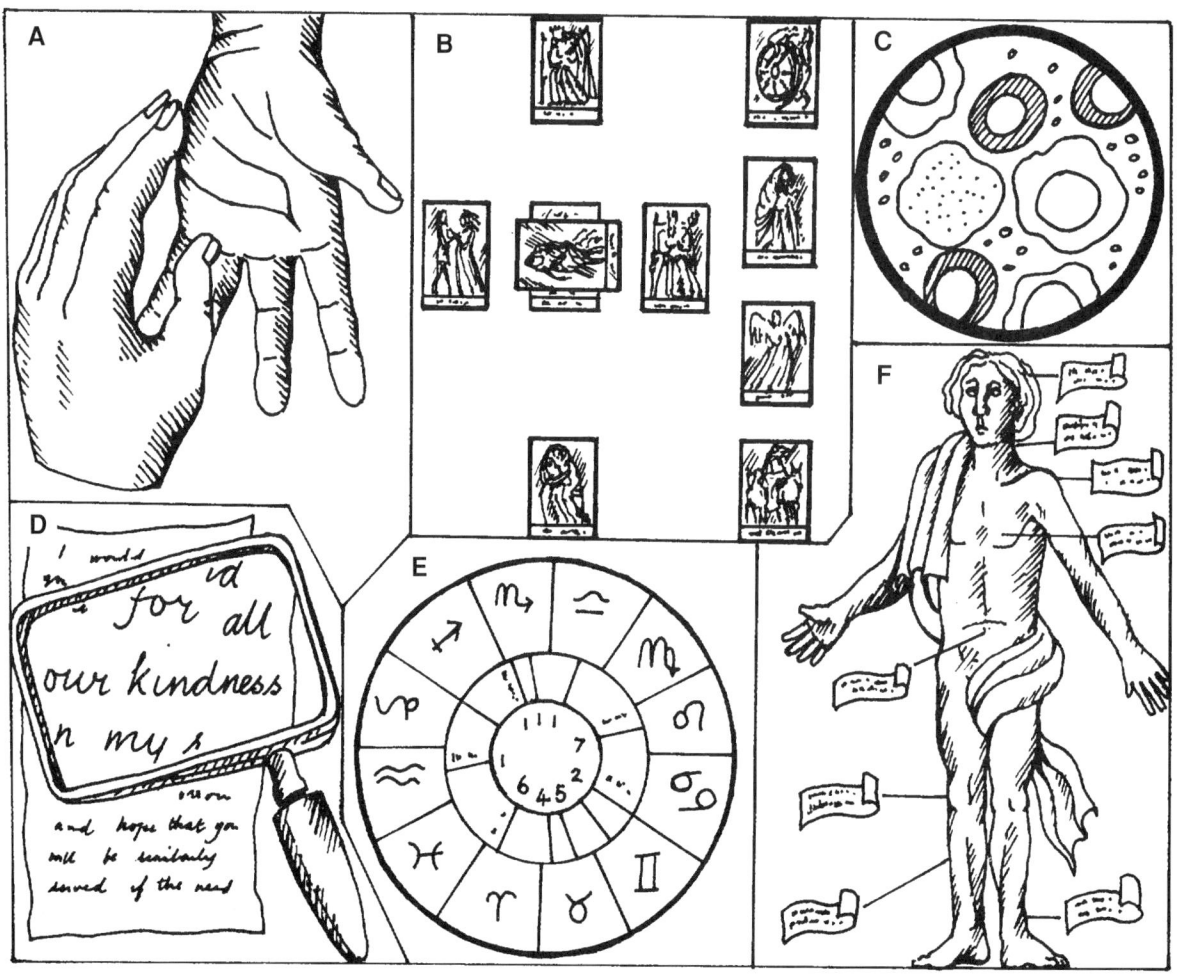

3 Try this psychological test. Choose the view that you like most and then read the description of your character underneath. Do you agree with the assessment of your character?

Read the other descriptions. Do they apply to you more than the one you read? Do you think this sort of test is accurate?

A You want to escape from your present life to seek adventure in another country. For you the sea is a symbol of freedom, but it also gives you a sense of security – a sense that there is something that never changes. However, although you want to escape, you are also dependant on other people; you need your friends. You are difficult to live with, but at the same time you are tender. In love you have a lot to offer, but also you demand too much from your partner.

B You are a serious person and like to base your life on definite ideas and values. At the same time you are ambitious and the mountains represent a challenge for you; you have a strong desire to do well and succeed. You like the outdoor life and hate wasting time. In love you expect something fantastic – you are not satisfied with something that is second best.

C You are an imaginative and creative person. The hills stimulate your imagination and sometimes lead you to daydreaming instead of concentrating on the matter in hand. You are an affectionate person and enjoy the company of a lot of people around you. In love you are sentimental and romantic, but you must be careful not to trust others too much or to look for something which isn't there.

D You do not like to be alone, but prefer the company of other people – especially those who are similar to yourself. You feel protected in small groups and look for people who share the same ideas as you. Rooves represent somewhere to hide away from the problems and difficulties of the world. You are a good and faithful friend – someone that people can trust.

E You are a person who is always looking for action, you want things to happen – but sometimes you want an easy solution when there isn't one. You look for order and logic in everything, even in love. You don't have much imagination, but you are very practical and have skills that other people envy. In love you are suspicious of very strong emotions. You prefer something less exciting but more stable.

F You feel the need to achieve strong results and will spend any amount of money to achieve your desired objectives. You are fascinated by destiny, but you don't give in to it easily. You like to keep up to date and have an interest in fashion. You are a leader – you weren't born to follow the others like a sheep. Big cities represent for you places where you have the space to act. In love you look for stability and an uncomplicated relationship. You don't trust sentimentality and you don't allow yourself to be led by unrealisable dreams.

H OMEWORK

You have been asked to write the horoscope for a newspaper. Your editor wants you to choose one sign (not your own) and predict what will happen in the coming months. You should include as many of the topics below as possible.

family life money work romance health entertainment travel study friends

16 In the Antarctic

In 1985 Robert Swan led a trip to the South Pole. He wanted to retrace the steps of the famous British explorer Captain Scott who, in 1912, finally reached the South Pole after a long and difficult journey. Swan travelled 1 500 kilometres over snow and ice in extremely cold temperatures (as low as –30 degrees Celsius). He later wrote about his experience in a book called *Antarctic Survival*.

1 These are some of the things that Robert Swan took on his trip. Label the picture using the words below.

skis
sledge
rucksack
sleeping bag
tent
stove
anorak

2 Here are two extracts from Swan's book *Antarctic Survival*. Find the following information from the first extract.

a What items of food and drink does he mention?
b How many calories a day did they exist on?
c Why couldn't they drink tea?
d How far did they plan to travel per day?
e How much did their sledges weigh at the beginning of the trip?

DAILY ROUTINE

Each day was the same. The alarm went at 7.00 am and one of us got up to light the stove for breakfast. We had to have an alarm; we were getting so tired that without it we would have slept until midday.

Breakfast was hot chocolate, biscuits, butter and oatmeal blocks. Then we got up, stuffed away our sleeping bags, cleared out the tent, collapsed it, packed the sledges, put on our skis, and set off. Once we had finished breakfast, we had to move quickly or else we would have got cold. We set off taking it in turns to lead, three hours at a time. Navigation was simple; we had chosen a direct route once we were past Minna Bluff. We knew our compass bearing. From time to time the person leading stopped and sighted on a distant distinctive patch of snow or even part of a cloud and then walked towards it, pausing now and then to check. At the end of three hours, the leader stopped and the others caught up, and we had a hot drink from the Thermoses. Then another three hours and a stop for lunch. That was soup, biscuits, butter, salami and chocolate. We needed all the energy we could get so we ate lots of fat, including a quarter kilo of butter a day! We had worked out supplies for a 5 100 calories a day diet but still lost weight on the journey – but disproved the theories of experts who had said we would need 8 000 calories per day. Three more hours after lunch and we stopped for 'tea'. Alas no tea, only more chocolate. Tea bags are heavy and do not give any calories, so we had to do without. And then on for another hour before making camp. We had to make an average of 16 kilometres a day in order to reach the South Pole in 90 days. That was all we had food for. But we also had to conserve our energy, we must take it easy and not rush during those early days. We started with our sledges weighing 160 kilos and you cannot hurry with that sort of weight!

3 What is it really like walking across the Antarctic hour after hour? Read the second extract and decide how many of the following he complains of. Which line in the text gives you the information?

hunger	boredom
disease	tiredness
thirst	animals
pain	

TEDIUM

And so the days passed. On 14 November, eleven days out from Scott Base, we passed the 160 kilometre mark. We skied along, the conversation long since dried up. Talking makes you thirsty and skiing was already thirsty work. Each of us
5 were thinking different thoughts. It is very boring to ski along with nothing to look at. To overcome this problem, I used to walk through the streets of London – the only trouble with this was that when I imagined passing a restaurant I would immediately start thinking of food, and I would wonder what
10 was on the menu! We were always hungry.

The worst bit of all was leading in a white-out. Out there, it would easily happen. The sky and the snow merge and there is no horizon. The feeling was of walking inside a ping-pong ball and it was very tiring. We had only the compass to give us
15 a sense of direction, and sometimes we began to doubt that.

Gareth and I both began to suffer from sore feet, and we had to spend time and attention looking after them in the evenings. Our feet were desperately important in succeeding and we had to look after them. Fortunately
20 mine healed but unluckily Gareth's did not, and he suffered agony.

4 Where could you go in your country for a 36 hour walking expedition including a night out in a tent? Plan an itinerary for a group of six people including times of departure and arrival. Make a list of essential equipment that you will need to take with you.

HOMEWORK

Write a short leaflet advertising the trip including the list of essential equipment and a map of the route that will be taken.

17 Ky Ho

1 Ky Ho is a very unusual person. This article was written about him in a local newspaper. Read the article and answer the questions below.

a Where is Ky Ho from?
b When did he leave his country?
c How did he manage to get his parents to Britain?
d Where is he studying now?
e Which school subjects is he particularly good at?
f What does he hope to do in the future?
g What does he like doing in his spare time?

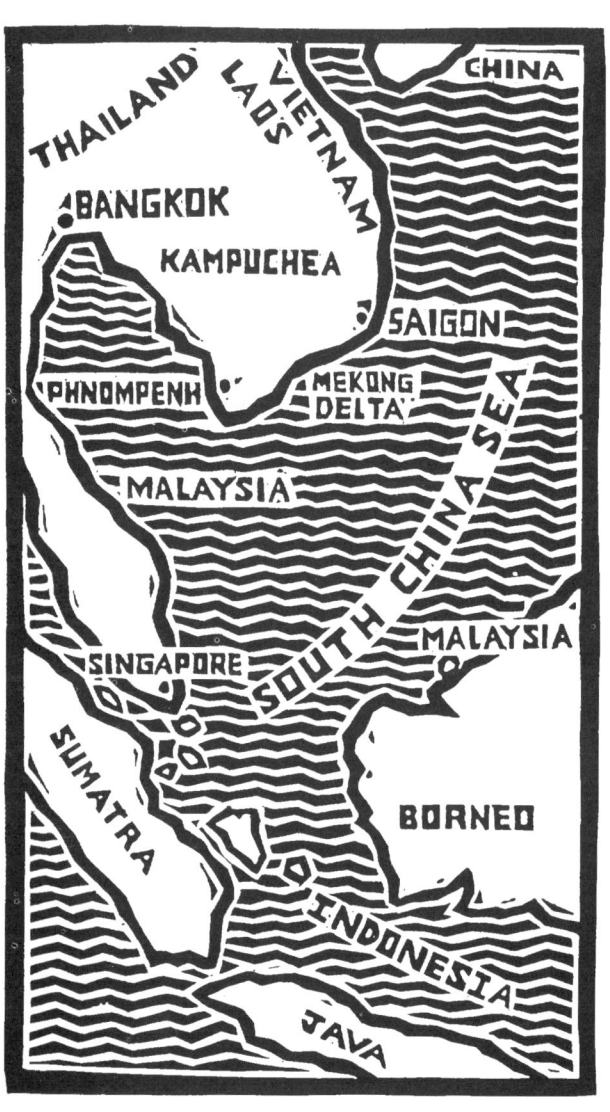

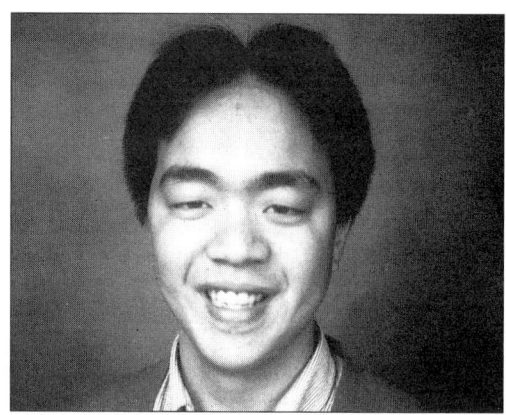

A Boat Boy at Millfield

Vietnamese Boat Boy Ky Ho, aged 18, has won a free scholarship to the country's most expensive public school. Ky has just started his sixth form studies at the famous Millfield School, on a two year course worth £12 000.

Just five years ago, speaking no English, he left Saigon with 120 other refugees on a nightmare trip to Singapore, leaving behind his parents and five brothers and sisters. Ky promised his father, Mr To Ho, he would reunite his family somehow, and last January they came together for the first time. Ky wrote to the Home Office, the Prime Minister and his own government to achieve his aim.

Ky's journey to England, in a cramped boat, nearly ended in disaster when storms forced the refugees to return to the notorious Mekong Delta, where they had to hide. But eventually, navigating with a school atlas and a ruler, they reached Malaysia and were taken in tow by the Royal Navy.

Ky quickly proved his abilities at Harlech Comprehensive and at Newton High School, where he passed nine 'O' levels this summer, including four A grades. Millfield offered him a place after learning of his exceptional talents in mathematics and science and he is likely to gain a place at either Oxford or Cambridge. He plans to make a career in computers and electronics and already owns his own computer.

A spokesman at the school said yesterday, "At Millfield he is seen as a quiet, unassuming Chinese boy who makes friends easily. " His hobbies, not inappropriately, are canoe building and sailing.

2 Using the text to help you, match the words with the definitions below.

a nightmare
b canoe
c atlas
d scholarship
e refugee
f navigating

(i) a free place at a school or university
(ii) somebody who leaves their country because of war or famine
(iii) a bad dream
(iv) finding the route you have to take when you are in a plane or ship
(v) a book containing maps of the world
(vi) a type of boat for one or two people made of wood or fibre glass

3 Imagine you are a journalist. Your editor has asked you to write an article about Ky's escape from Vietnam which must include the details below.

Date of departure from Vietnam
Reasons for his escape
Details of the boat and the conditions on it
Details of life on the island
Date of arrival in Britain

4 Listen to the interview and make notes on the information you will need for the article.

Make sure you have got the correct information by comparing your answers with another student.

H OMEWORK

Write the article that your editor has asked for.

18 Castaway

1 Look at this picture of a desert island. You are alone on the island and you have nothing with you. Invent a story about how you got there.

2 How many things can you identify in the picture?

Label the picture using the words below.

beach   well   stream
wave   rocks   sea
hut   cave   raft
mountain   bush   canoe
palm tree

3 Would you enjoy being a castaway on a desert island? What would be the advantages and disadvantages of such a life? Discuss the following questions with another student.

What problems would you have?
How would you survive?
Would you try to escape? How?
How would you spend your time?

4 If you could take one of each of the following things, what would you choose?

a cassette
a book
a useful object
a luxury item
an animal

5

Ted Zapp is lead singer of the group *Fizz*. He was born on a train (the trans-Siberian express) in 1963. Since this unusual start to life he has continued to shock those around him. He was expelled from school at the age of 15 and then got a job as a waiter on a large ship and went round the world. For a while he was a taxi driver in Sydney, Australia and then worked as a model in America before coming back to Britain where he formed the group *Fizz* which has been so successful with its first three records.

Listen to Ted Zapp talking about his selection on the local radio programme Castaway. What does he choose to take with him to the island?

a cassette   a luxury item
a book   an animal
a useful object

HOMEWORK

You want to communicate your experiences to the outside world. Write a message to put in a bottle. Include details of how you got to the island, your life on the island, what you miss and whether you want to be rescued or not.

19 Renting a Room

1 In England many people let rooms in their houses to people who need somewhere to live. The people pay money for this and are called lodgers.

How would you feel about living in someone else's house? What advantages and disadvantages would there be?

How would you feel about having a lodger living in your own house? What are the advantages and disadvantages of this?

2 **Role Play**
Renting a Room

STUDENT A
Imagine you want to let a room in your house to a lodger. Read the advice *Questions to ask your lodger* and make a list of questions you want to ask anybody who comes to see you. You will also need to think of the rules you want to have in your house. Then ask Student B these questions and decide if you think he/she would be a suitable person to have in the house.

STUDENT B
Imagine you want to rent a room in a house. Read the advice *Questions to ask your landlord/landlady* and make a list of questions you want to ask. Then ask Student A these questions and decide if you would like to live in his/her house.

QUESTIONS TO ASK YOUR LODGER

It's perfectly acceptable to ask your prospective lodger for references, either from people who know them, from previous landlords or from their bank.

Although there are certain questions which can tell you a lot, much will depend on how well you get on with the person. If you have any doubts, don't say yes.

When you interview your prospective lodger, make out a checklist of questions before you start talking. Here are some guidelines on what to ask.

Interests: it's usually a good idea to find out about a lodger's hobbies before they move in, or you may find you have a keen violinist practising until all hours!

Friends: it's unusual nowadays to stop people inviting their friends to the house, but if it worries you, make it clear you're not keen on late-night parties, or people staying the night without prior warning.

Smoking: if you really can't bear smoke, you must make it clear that you don't allow any smoking in specified rooms of your home.

Pets: find out whether the lodger has any pets or intends keeping them – your *own* lease, if you have one, may stop you keeping animals in the house.

Payment: once you've agreed a rent that suits both sides, establish a regular payment system, perhaps through a bank standing order.

Chores: work out in advance how you're going to handle the household chores. You may choose to be totally responsible for cleaning, in which case you should take account of this in assessing the rent. However, many house-sharers prefer to work on a rota basis.

House Rules: if you're too dogmatic about what your lodger can and can't do, you're unlikely to have a happy relationship. But you can and should set some house rules in the interview if certain things are particularly important to you.

Future Plans: it's worth asking how long your lodger intends to stay, so you can plan ahead if it's only going to be for a short time.

QUESTIONS TO ASK YOUR LANDLORD/LANDLADY

It's difficult to live with someone you don't know. It's worth spending some time speaking to your landlord/landlady – especially with the aim of finding out the house rules – before you make up your mind if you want to stay there or not. Make a checklist of questions before your interview. Here are some guidelines on what to ask landlords/landladies.

Friends: some are fairly strict about friends who come to the house. You need to find out whether friends can visit you in your room and secondly whether they can stay the night or not – although not many landlords/landladies are likely to allow this.

Housework: you need to establish whether you are expected to do any housework beyond keeping your room clean. If you are expected to contribute to the housework, then you might be able to negotiate a reduction in the rent.

The Bathroom: Many people are very possessive about their bathrooms. You need to establish if there is any particular time when you can or can't use the bathroom. Make sure you find out how often you are allowed to have a bath.

The Kitchen: the same rules apply for the kitchen. It is quite reasonable to expect to be able to use the kitchen to cook your own food. It's either that or a permanent diet of take away pizzas and kebabs!

Noise: Are there any rules about playing your stereo at certain times? Also, can you watch the house TV?

The Telephone: It's vital to get this one right! A lot of arguments have occurred because the rules about the telephone haven't been properly understood. Find out if you can use the telephone for outgoing calls and what the system of recording and paying for these calls is. Does your landlord/landlady mind if other people ring you at the house? Up to what time?

Smoking: Again, it's hopeless thinking you are going to get on if one of you smokes and the other doesn't.

3 Read this advertisement.

> Large room to let in detached house near the centre of Bristol. Central heating, shared kitchen and bathroom. £195 per month. Ring 0272 493852. Evenings.

Now listen to this conversation between the landlord of the house advertised and a possible lodger. Make notes on what he says about the following.

the bathroom
the kitchen
having parties
the telephone
smoking
music and television
towels, sheets and blankets

4 Later the landlord wrote to the lodger enclosing a list of the house rules. The landlord has obviously changed his mind about some of the rules! How many differences can you notice between what he said and what he wrote?

> RULES OF THE HOUSE
>
> * You will be issued with your own keys, but these must not be given to anybody else.
> * It is forbidden to listen to music or watch television after 10.30.
> * You are only allowed one bath a day. This must be taken between 6.00 pm and 8.00 pm.
> * The kitchen can only be used before 8.00 am and after 7.30 pm.
> * Smoking is not allowed anywhere in the house.
> * It is strictly forbidden to have parties in the house.
> * Lodgers are expressly forbidden to have friends to stay overnight.
> * You may receive incoming calls only.
> * You are requested to bring your own sheets and towels. Blankets will be provided.
>
> D. Galway

HOMEWORK

Imagine you have agreed to let a friend stay in your house/flat while you are away on holiday. Write a note to him/her to explain where everything is and what your friend should/shouldn't do.

20 A Place to Live

1 Which of the following are important for you when selecting somewhere to live? Mark them like this:

1 very important
2 quite important
3 not important

a lot of space
plenty of natural light
good views
a garden
a modern kitchen
a quiet area
a modern bathroom with a shower
pleasant neighbours
shops nearby
close to public transport
in the centre of a town
in the country
near a school

Compare your ideas with another student.
Have you got the same ideas?

2 Listen to an estate agent showing someone round a house. As you listen, look at the plan of the house and decide which part of the house the letters refer to. The first one has been done for you.

ground floor		first floor	
a	the hall	**g**	
b		**h**	
c		**i**	
d		**j**	
e			
f			

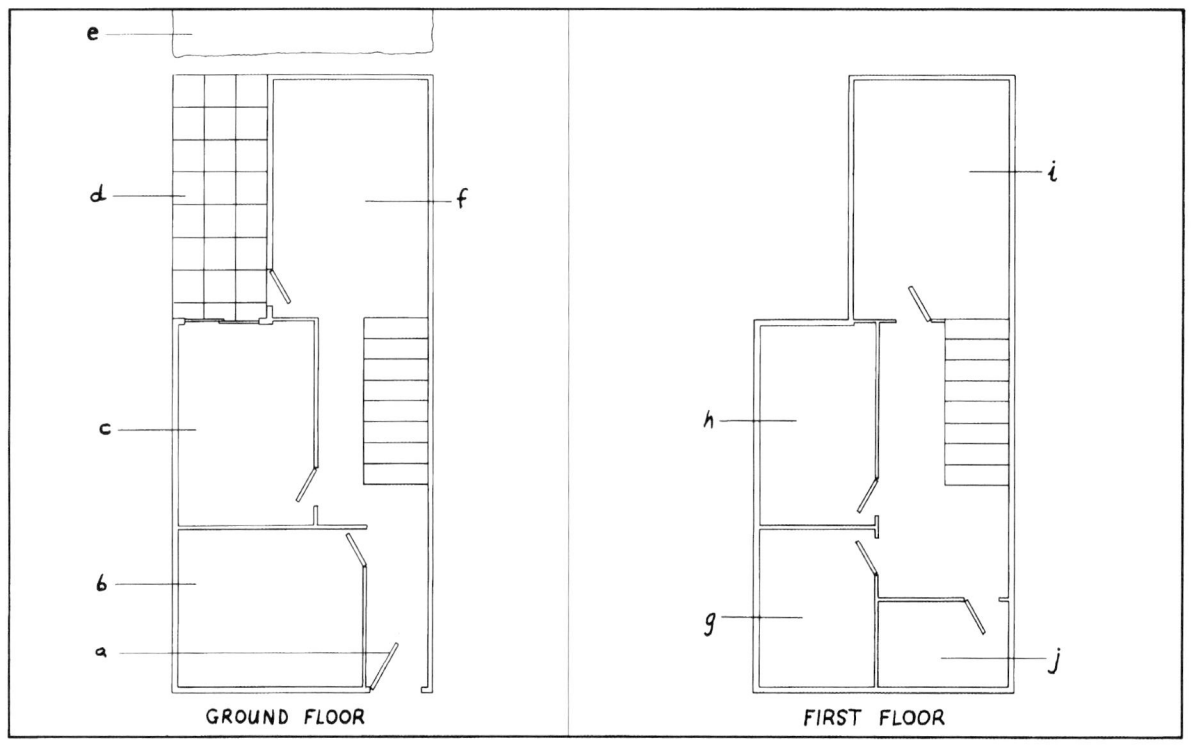

GROUND FLOOR   FIRST FLOOR

HISTORY 2.

40

3 Listen to the estate agent again. Which of the following features does he mention?

a large garden
central heating
convenient for buses

near a sports centre
near a good school
near the centre of town

large bathroom
in a quiet area
thick, solid walls

4 **Role Play**
Buying a House

STUDENT A
You are looking for a house on the main road between a small village called Chrome and a large town called Winton. There are only three houses for sale. Talk to the three owners about the houses, ask any questions you want and choose which one you would most like to buy.

STUDENT B
You are the owner of *Chez Nous*.

STUDENT C
You are the owner of *Hill View*.

STUDENT D
You are the owner of *Home Sweet Home*.

The owner should convince the buyer that his/her house is the best one. Try to point out the best features of your house and try to hide the worst features.

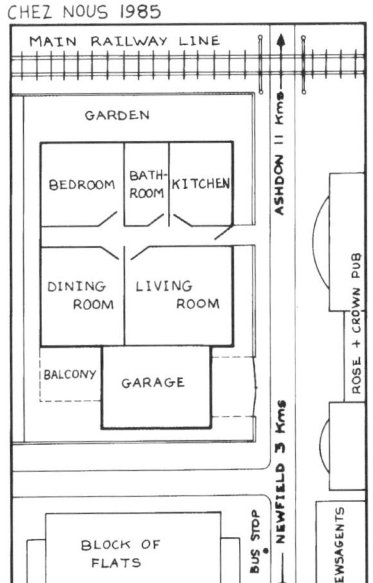

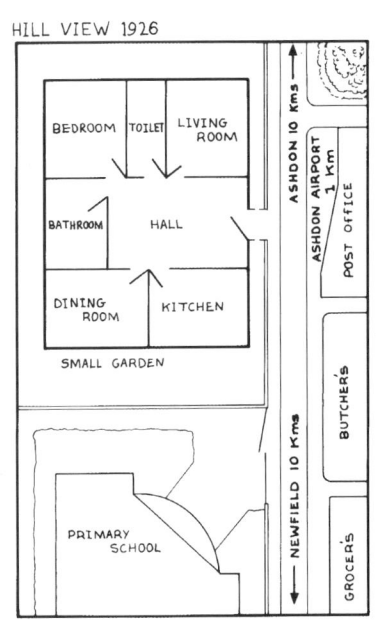

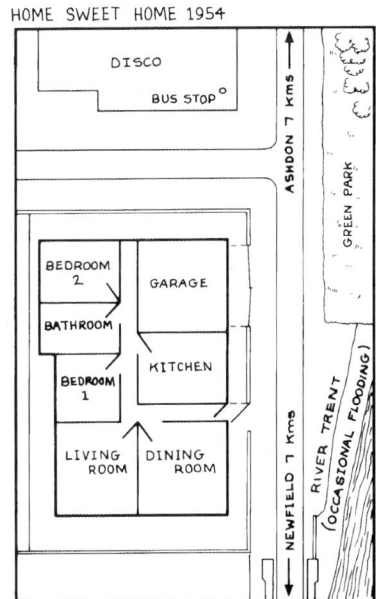

HOMEWORK

Imagine you want to sell the house you live in at the moment. Write a description of the house which exaggerates its good features.

21 My Dream House

1 Which of these places would you most like to live in? Why? What are the advantages of living there?

Where would you least like to live? What are the disadvantages of living there?

2 Some years ago Mr Pedley set up a business which was extremely successful, so he and his wife bought this house.

3 What do you think of it? Would you like to live there? Can you think of any disadvantages of living in a house like this?

Listen to Mrs Pedley talking about their house and answer these questions.

a When did she move there?
b How many bedrooms are there?
c How many people does she employ to help her look after the house?
d What was Mr Pedley's old job?
e Why did he leave this job?
f What does Mr Pedley do now?
g What else have they bought with their money?

4 Would you like to be rich? Can you think of any disadvantages of being rich? How would you spend your money? Which of the following would you do if you suddenly won a large amount of money?

buy a luxury house
buy a boat
invest it
buy things for your relatives
buy a fast car
give some of it to charity
go travelling round the world

5 Design your own dream house.
If you had an unlimited amount of money and could design a house as you wanted, what would it be like? With another student, try to agree on a dream house. Consider the following points.

The place Where would it be situated?

The surroundings What would you see from the bedroom windows?

The size How many floors? How many rooms?

The age Would you prefer an old house or a brand new one?

Luxuries A swimming pool? A tennis court? A field for the horse? What luxuries would you include?

HOMEWORK

Write a description of your house using illustrations where necessary.

---

22 Training

1 Are you taking enough exercise?

Ask another student about the amount of exercise he/she takes per week. Ask the following questions.

How often do you take exercise in a week?
How long do you exercise each time?
What sort of exercise is it?

Do you think he/she takes enough exercise?

What advice would you give him/her?

2 Which of the following sports do you think are the best for keeping fit? Think of strength, suppleness and stamina.

running	gymnastics
golf	football
basketball	weight lifting
tennis	badminton
swimming	

3 How much do you know about the Marathon? Do this quiz.

MARATHON QUIZ

A long time ago a messenger ran a great distance between two cities to bring news of a battle to his masters.

1 When did this happen?

900 BC	490 BC
120 BC	270 AD

2 In which country did this happen?

Turkey Greece Italy Spain

3 Marathon was:

the name of one of the cities.
the name of the king.
the name of the messenger.

4 What is the approximate distance of the modern marathon?

25 kilometres	42 kilometres
54 kilometres	66 kilometres

5 What is the approximate world record time?

1 hour 40 mins	2 hours 8 mins
2 hours 35 mins	3 hours 27 mins

---

4 Read the following passage and answer these questions.

   a How long before a Marathon should you start training?
   b How many kilometres per week should you run at the start of the programme?
   c How many kilometres should you run in the last week before the start of a race?
   d Should you drink during the race?
   e What should you do immediately after a race?
   f What should you do the next day?

Running a Marathon

Nowadays thousands of people run marathons each year. But each athlete has to prepare his or her mind and body to run the marathon in one go.

The purpose of training

Training is necessary to make the body work harder than it is used to. A good club runner begins to prepare for a Marathon at least three months ahead. Preparation includes races, many hours of planned running at different speeds and changes in diet. During the training period the runner must eat a regular and balanced diet. The diet should include a lot of carbohydrates to supply the energy required in training.

The Training Schedule

In the early days, runners will cover 80 kilometres per week. The weekly total is increased every two or three weeks and at least two long runs per week are added. Simple 'loosening up' exercises must be used before and after running. These exercises help the body to prepare for running and to return to normal afterwards.

Final Preparations

Two weeks before the Marathon, the training programme is reduced. If 100 kilometres per week have been covered, this will be reduced to 60 kilometres and then to 30 kilometres in the final week. On the last two days there may be no running at all. Some runners change their diet during the final week.

Race Day

Breakfast should be eaten at least three hours before the race. Food which can easily be digested such as cereal, toast and scrambled egg is suitable, with as much fluid as possible. A further $250 \ cm^3$ at least of water should be drunk about half an hour before the race to keep up the body fluid levels.

Along the route runners can use the feeding stations placed about every five kilometres. They provide water, dilute fruit juice and special drinks. The rule is to drink little but often. Between feeding stations are sponging stations. Runners cool themselves by sponging down their faces, necks and thighs.

Controlling body heat is a big problem for a Marathon runner. About 20 times more heat is being produced during a Marathon than when at rest. As much as 1 kg of fluid may be lost. If the weather is hot and humid, sweat will not evaporate and heat will build up in the body. This could produce overheating and cause serious fatigue, dizziness and possible collapse.

After the race

After the race, the runner must be kept warm by putting on a track suit or using a space blanket. Above all, the runner must keep moving, even slowly, to stop himself from getting stiff. A lot of drink must be taken for two to three hours after a race, and a meal rich in carbohydrates is needed to restore energy reserves.

On the day after, a jog for a couple of kilometres or so is advised. Then four to five kilometres are jogged on the following, and so on. Jogging helps the body to move properly again and to remove waste products from the muscles. Soon all stiffness and weariness disappears and the runner is ready to prepare for the next race.

HOMEWORK

Complete the following poster giving advice to athletes in training for a Marathon using information from the text.

HOW TO WIN A MARATHON

Training

1 Start training three months before the start of a race

2

3

4

Race Day

1 Eat your breakfast three hours before the start of the race.

2

3

After the race

1 Keep moving after the race.

2

23 Getting Started

1 Mike Trees is an expert on running. He is going to give some advice to people who want to take up jogging.

What advice do you think he will give to a beginner? Consider the following headings.

Distance
Clothes and shoes
Getting ready
Eating
The benefits of running

2 Listen to Mike and make notes on what he says about each topic.

Did you have the same ideas?

3 Label the picture using the words in the list below.

ankle	heel	shoulder
calf	hip	sole
foot	knee	thigh
head	neck	trunk

4 Mike talked about the need to do warm-up exercises before going running. Here are some of the stretching exercises that he recommends. Match the description of the excercises with the diagrams.

WARMING UP
Start your warm-up by jogging for about 800 m. Then move on to some gentle exercises like the ones shown here, to stretch your muscles. You should hold each stretch for about five seconds and then relax before repeating it.

1 Trunk muscles
Raise your left arm above your head and bend to the right. Avoid leaning forwards or backwards. Hold for five seconds, then straighten up. Repeat five times on each side.

2 Hamstrings
Stand on your left leg and support your right leg on a chair. Keeping both legs straight, stretch forward and hold your right foot, or as far down your leg as you can reach. Hold for five seconds and repeat five times on each leg.

3 Calf muscles
Stand in front of a wall and take one stride backwards. Lean forwards and place your hands against the wall. keeping your body straight, press your heels to the floor, stretching your calf muscles, repeat five times.

4 Ankles
Sit with your right leg stretched out in front of you. Hold your left leg in your arms so that the lower leg hangs loosely, then rotate your left foot ten times in each direction. Repeat with the other foot.

5 Shoulder muscles
Holding your arms straight, swing them gently in large circular movements. Swing your arms forwards for about ten seconds, then swing them backwards.

6 Inside of thighs
Sit on the floor and place the soles of your feet together. Pull your feet up towards your body. Then gently press your knees down towards the floor. Repeat five times.

7 Lower back muscles
Lie face-down on the floor, with your hands under your shoulders. Keeping your hips on the ground, look up at the ceiling and push up to raise your upper body. Repeat five times.

WARMING DOWN
Always remember to warm down at the end of your run. Start your warm-down with some easy stretching exercises like the ones shown above. Move on to some gentle jogging.

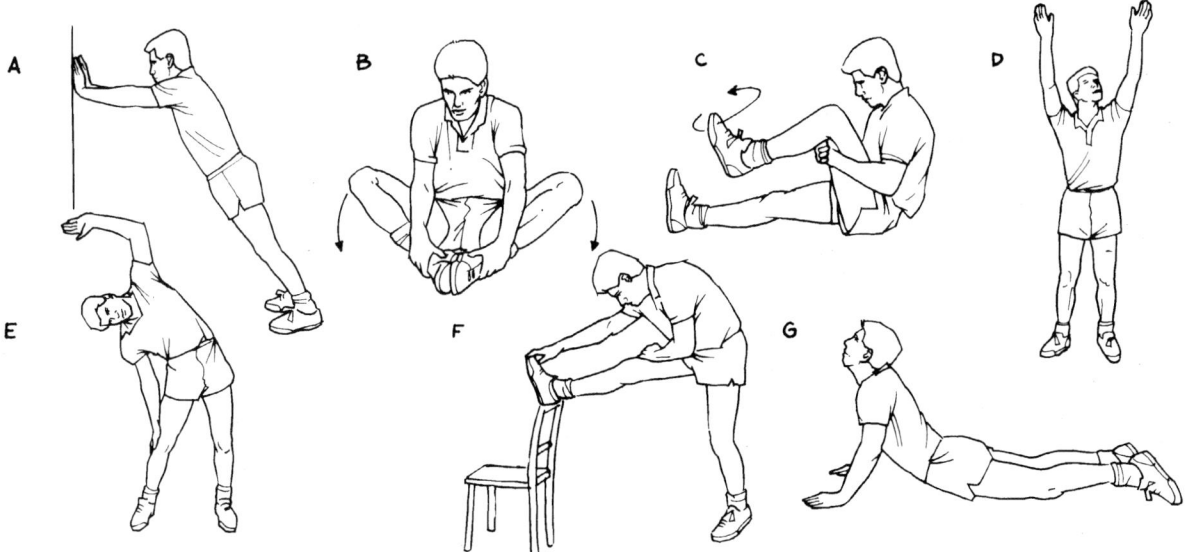

A   B   C   D

E   F   G

24 Sumo Wrestling

1 Look at the photograph of these men.

Where are they?
What are they doing?
Where are they from?
What's your reaction to their size?

2 Sumo wrestling is an ancient Japanese sport. Read the description of Sumo opposite and answer these questions.

    a How long do tournaments last in Japan?
    b How long does a fight usually last?
    c Can women take part in this sport?
    d Why do they clap their hands before a fight?
    e Why is it important for them to rest after a meal?
    f How old are they when they start their training?

SUMO

Tournaments

The Sumo wrestling that can be seen today dates back to the Edo period (1603 – 1868). Nowadays there are tournaments in Japan six times a year. Each tournament (called a *basho*) lasts 15 days. Only men can take part, although hundreds of years ago women also fought. It is almost only the Japanese who take part, but in 1972 Jesse Kuhaulua, who was born in Hawaii, won an important tournament.

Rituals

There are many rituals that have to be carried out before the fight can start. The wrestlers stamp the ground to frighten away any evil spirits and clap their hands to attract the attention of the Gods. They also throw salt which is to purify both the wrestlers and the ring. Before the fight, they extend their hands to show that they are not hiding any weapons and stare at each other for a long time. These rituals before a fight often take many minutes and are part of the psychological build-up designed to frighten each other.

The fight

The fight itself is very short, usually lasting only a few seconds. It is very rare for a fight to go on longer than a minute. The aim is for one wrestler to move the other out of the ring or *dohyo*. The wrestlers have to accept the decision of the referee – there is no arguing. If, however, it is difficult to decide who was pushed out of the ring first, the referee can order a rematch. When fighting the wrestlers wear a brightly coloured *mawashi* – a type of belt made of silk.

The wrestlers

Sumo wrestlers are extremely large but very fit men. They are often 1.80 m tall and can easily weigh up to 136 kgs. During their training they learn how to cook and are responsible for their own diet. Traditionally they eat *chankonabe* which is a dish of meat or fish with vegetables, usually served with rice. They drink large quantities of beer which helps them to put on weight, but drunkeness is not encouraged. After their meals the wrestlers usually have a rest so that the food and drink can turn to fat. They start their training quite young (12 or 13) and gradually hope to work up to the highest level – *Yokozuna* – that of Grand Champion, but only about 60 wrestlers have ever attained this level. They usually retire in their 30s and then lose weight. Most of them live to a good old age.

3 The following words are all terms used in Sumo wrestling. Read the text again and find out what they mean.

basho   *chankonabe*
dohyo   *yokozuna*
mawashi

4 Discuss the statement below with some other students. Use the questions that follow to guide your discussion.

Boxing is the only sport I know where the aim of the competitors is to hurt each other as much as possible. It is an aggressive and dangerous sport and, therefore, should be banned.

Do you agree with the statement?
What are the arguments against boxing?
Can you think of any arguments in support of boxing?
What do you feel about other sports which are dangerous or cruel? Look at the following list. Would you ban any of these?

motor racing
hunting animals for sport
bull fighting
fishing
judo

Now find out the opinion of the rest of the group.

HOMEWORK

Choose a sport you are interested in. Find out as much as you can about the history and rules of the sport and write a description of the sport.

25 Snakes

How much do you know about snakes?

1 Work with a partner and try to answer these questions. If you don't know, have a guess.

a How fast can a snake travel?
b What is the maximum length of a snake?
c What do snakes eat?
d What is the most dangerous country for snakes?
e Can you name two poisonous snakes?
f Can you name two snakes which kill their victims by squeezing them (constriction)?

2 Read this passage and find the answers to the questions in **1**.

There are many different species of snake (over 2 500) and they are found in all parts of the world except the Arctic and Antarctic, New Zealand, Ireland and most of Polynesia. Of these about 400 kinds are venomous including cobras, coral snakes and kraits.

Snakes are classified as reptiles although they have no legs and no eyelids. They have nostrils but use these to breathe through rather than smell with. The sense of smell is well developed but on the whole they use their tongues to give themselves information about their surroundings.

Despite what people think, snakes are not cold and slimy to touch but have a dry skin. This skin is renewed several times a year – a process known as *sloughing*. They move by wriggling from side to side but cannot travel very fast – about 12 kms per hour over level ground. Snakes vary considerably in size. The biggest is the anaconda which can reach 13 metres followed by the rock python which can measure from 9 – 10 metres.

The majority of snakes lay eggs but others, such as boas and rattlesnakes, give birth to live young. These young are able to look after themselves from the moment they are born. In mild and cold areas snakes hibernate in the winter months seeking shelter in caves or underground. Most snakes cannot tolerate temperatures below 100 Celsius. Snakes are carnivorous feeding on rats, mice, frogs, birds, lizards and fish. They can swallow animals considerably wider than their own heads because the bones of the jaw are movable. Some snakes eat their prey alive but others kill their victims first either by poisoning them or by squeezing them to death.

Snakes do not usually attack man but will defend themselves if threatened. Venomous snakes use special teeth to inject poison into their victims. The most deadly poison comes from sea-snakes found in the Western Pacific and Indian Oceans. India is a particularly dangerous country for poisonous snakes, having cobras, kraits and the large Russell's viper. About 15 000 to 20 000 people are killed there each year partly because so many people walk around bared-footed.

3 Richard has an unusual hobby. He keeps snakes as pets. Listen to him talking about his snakes and answer these questions.

a Which of the following snakes has he got?

viper	rattlesnake
python	boa constrictor
mamba	cobra
grass snake	krait

b Which of the following does a snake need?

to be kept warm/to be kept cool
a big enclosure/a small enclosure
plenty of water/a little water
food every day/food twice a week

c What do his snakes eat?

d How much does an average size snake cost?

4 You are going to hear a radio phone-in where listeners ask experts questions. This week the expert is a doctor who specialises in the kind of problems that you might meet when travelling.

a The first caller, Mrs Rushton, asks for advice on how to treat exposure to the cold (hypothermia). As you listen, put the following instructions in the same order as they are given on the programme.

Cover with blankets.
Don't give any alcohol.
Consult a doctor if the condition appears serious.
Warm the person.
Remove any wet clothing and dry the person.
Give warm food and drink.

b Listen to the next caller's question and make notes on what to do if someone gets bitten by a poisonous snake.

H OMEWORK

Write a set of instructions for dealing with a poisonous snake bite.

26 World Problems

1 What does the cartoon below suggest to you? Who do you think was responsible for drawing it?

2 a Dr Lawton is an expert on the environment. He is giving a talk on the environment and the individual. Listen to the talk. Which of the following does he mention?

saving energy
recycling glass and paper
acid rain
joining an action group
the destruction of rain forests
the ozone layer
solar energy
using lead-free petrol
buying organic food

b Listen to the talk again and answer these questions.

  (i) List three ways of saving energy
  (ii) What are the two advantages of using lead free petrol?
  (iii) Which two action groups does he mention?

3 Compare your answers in **2** with another student. Using the information from the talk, design a poster for your college or school with advice to other students who want to help.

4 **a** Look at these cartoons which are taken from *The Friends of the Earth Handbook* and think of a sentence to go with each one.

b Read the introductory leaflet on *Friends of the Earth*. Work with another student and discuss what measures could be taken to prevent the problems it mentions.

The Earth needs all the friends it can get. And it needs them now. For thousands upon thousands of years, our planet has sustained a wonderfully rich tapestry of life. Now, one single species – humankind – is putting the Earth at risk.

People the world over are suffering the effects of pollution, deforestation and radiation. Species are disappearing at a terrifying rate. The warming of the atmosphere threatens us all with devastating changes in climate and food production.

It needn't be like this. We know enough to reverse the damage, and to manage the Earth's astonishing wealth more fairly and sustainably. But the political will to bring about such a transformation is still lacking.

And that's exactly where Friends of the Earth comes in. Isn't it time you joined us?

Contact us at this address:
FRIENDS OF THE EARTH
26-28 Underwood Street
London N1 7JQ

HOMEWORK

Either draw a cartoon to illustrate some problem with the environment **or** write a four line poem to draw people's attention to an environmental problem.

27   Zoo

1   Which of the following words is the Odd Man Out in each group i.e. which is the word that doesn't fit in the group? Give a reason why it doesn't fit.

leopard	dog	lamb	bear	panda
lion	gorilla	chicken	horse	tiger
giraffe	seal	cow	elephant	whale
panther	rhinoceros	rat	camel	monkey

2   Look at this photograph. Discuss with another student why you think this whale was killed.

3 Write a list of all the things you can think of
that are made from animals. Which ones do
you think are justifiable?

4 What is your opinion of zoos? Make a list of
the arguments for and against zoos. Compare
your list with another student.

5 Kim Simmons helps to run a zoo in Linton.

Listen to her talking about her zoo. As you
listen, answer these questions.

a What are the two main aims of the zoo?
b Who started it?
c Which animals does she think may soon
become extinct?
d List two things made from animals that she
mentions.
e List four things they have to spend money
on at the zoo.

28 Looking Back

1 How much do you know about the past? Do this quiz.

---

1 The first flight across the Atlantic was in

   1850   1901   1919   1939

2 Passengers were first transported by train in

   1825   1865   1901   1925

3 Colour television was first broadcast in

   1945   1953   1962   1970

4 The first man went into space in

   1955   1959   1961   1969

5 The first telephone conversation took place in

   1876   1904   1926   1954

6 The modern bicycle was invented in

   1723   1845   1885   1904

7 The use of anaesthetics for an operation was first used in the

   1840's   1880's   1920's   1940's

---

2 Look at this photograph. What do you think life was like at that time? What were the advantages and disadvantages of living at that time?

3 Now listen to Emma talking about her life when she was young. Decide whether the following statements are true or false. If they are false, correct them.

a She had to sleep with her sisters in one room.
b She only had a bath once a week.
c There wasn't a toilet inside the house.
d The house felt very cold because there was no heating.
e She kept their food in the fridge.
f Her mother went shopping every day.
g She believes the weather was better when she was young.

Name three things she did in her free time.

4 Read this poem and answer the questions that follow.

Views of a Park

A child as big as a pebble,
Went skipping through the park,
Looking at every flower,
That once was me.

A girl as bright as summer,
Went wandering through the park,
In a world of wooded contentment,
That once was me.

A girl lost in a dream world,
Went strolling through the park,
All she wanted was quiet and a young man,
That once was me.

A woman struggling with luggage,
Went slowly through the park,
All she knew was noise and children,
That once was me.

An old woman in thoughtless mood,
Is sitting in the park,
All she asks is a bench and stillness,
That now is me.

Celia Ann Glover

pebble small stone
content happy
bench a long seat made of wood
to stroll to walk slowly
to struggle with to have difficulty with

Discuss these questions with another student.

How old is the woman now?

What do you think has happened to this woman in her life?

Has she had a good life?

Did she have a good childhood?

Did she get married?

Why did she walk through the park with luggage?

Do you think she had children?

What is her life like now?

HOMEWORK

Using your answers to the questions in **4**, write a short biography of Emma.

---

29 Memories of Childhood

1 What was your first memory? How old were you at the time? Ask another student about his/her first memory.

2 What sort of child were you? Which of the following can you remember doing?

- being rude to your parents
- smoking in secret
- drinking in secret
- leaving your room in a mess
- stealing from shops
- breaking things in the house
- leaving things out in the rain
- not doing your homework
- being rude to your teachers
- coming home late
- saying nasty things about your friends
- being cruel to animals

Score one mark for every 'yes' answer. Add up your marks

0–4   You were an angelic child – are you sure you are telling the truth?

5–7   You were a good child on the whole and one or two naughty moments were quite acceptable.

8–10   You were a naughty child – your friends may have liked you, but you caused problems for your parents and teachers.

11–12 You were impossible to live with – your parents and friends were in despair.

3 Read through the stories below quickly and find the correct title for each one.

a A Quick Way to Make Money
b A Friend is Wrongly Accused
c Girl Saved from Drowning
d Nobody Accepts Blame for Trick

Four people remember

Annie
I remember once when I was about eleven I got angry with a schoolfriend of mine, Sheila I think her name was, but I can't remember what she had done to annoy me. Anyway, I went round to her house one day with another friend and we saw these telephone wires running down the side of the house. We took the wires and tied them to the front door. Then we rang the doorbell and ran off to hide round the corner. Sheila's mother opened the door and the wires were pulled off the wall. They couldn't use the phone for three days. The funniest part was that Sheila's parents didn't know it was me that had done it and they wrote a letter to Jennifer's parents thinking it was her. Jennifer was another girl who lived in the same road. They never did discover that it was me!

David
I liked most of my teachers at school, but there was one teacher that we all hated – Mr Crabett. He was really strict and we were all frightened of him. He was tall, thin and had piercing eyes – eyes that always knew what we were doing. He always wore a grey suit and a bow tie and carried a walking stick with him wherever he went. He taught English and made us learn long poems by heart – we had to stand up and recite them one after the other, and if we couldn't remember them, we were given extra work or had to stay in after school until we had learned them.

He was so old-fashioned that he used a special pen that you have to dip into ink kept in a special ink-well 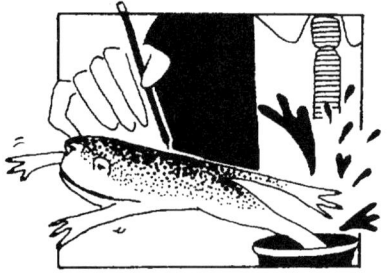 *in his desk. If ever anybody complained that something was unfair he would say, "Life is unfair; school is a training for life; therefore school must be unfair." We weren't allowed to argue with him!*

One day Mick arrived at school with a frog that he had found on the way to school. Mick was always getting into trouble with the teachers, but we liked him. The day he brought the frog to school he had a brilliant idea, but he made us agree that we would all be responsible if there was any trouble. We put the frog in Mr Crabett's ink-well just before he came into the class. Its head was just out of the ink, so it seemed quite happy.

Then Mr Crabett came in and sat down at his desk. He gave us some work to do and then took out his pen to mark his register. We all held our breath and looked up from our work.

"Well, get on with it", he barked. We went back to work. And then it happened, it really happened! For once in our lives we got the better of Mr Crabett. He dipped his pen in the ink, the nib of the pen hit the frog and the frog leaped out of the ink-well and hopped across the desk, splashing Mr. Crabett with ink. It went all over his white shirt and he was furious.

Keith

I remember I did do something very naughty once. I had been playing in the garden with a girlfriend who lived just down the road. At tea time we went into the kitchen and on the table we saw a tray full of flags – they were those flags that people buy for charity and then wear on their jackets or coats. My brother had been selling them for a charity, I can't remember which

one … but he hadn't sold all the flags. I thought it would be a good idea to sell them in the road and keep the money. So we took the flags and went down the road and knocked on peoples' doors. When they answered we asked them if they wanted to buy a flag. Usually they agreed and after about half an hour we had collected quite a lot of money. Then we made our mistake! We knocked on the door of our local schoolteacher – Miss North was her name. She realised that we didn't have the tin that people normally put the money in; so she rang up my father and asked him if he knew we were collecting money. He was furious! It was about the only time that he hit me.

Gillie

My first memory was really a bad one. I was nearly four years old and I was playing in the garden with a friend of mine. We got bored and started to walk along the canal, although we knew this was forbidden. Our dog came with us. My mother thought I was in my friend's garden next door, so she wasn't worried when she couldn't see me.

After a few minutes my friend, who was also very small, dared me to put my foot in the water of the canal. Well, of course, I fell into the canal which was filthy with dead rats and oil floating on it. My friend was frightened and ran home and didn't tell anyone about it. The dog started to bark and this drew the attention of someone looking out of a window of a factory on the other side of the canal. He opened the window and shouted to a man in the street to save me. The man jumped in and rescued me – only just in time for I had already gone under twice and was going down again for the third time when he fished me out.

I remember that I went home in an ambulance and when we arrived and my mother found out what had happened to me she fainted. They took us both to hospital. When I got there they made me drink salty water to make me sick to get rid of the dirty water that I had swallowed in the canal. However, my mother had to stay in hospital for shock treatment and I had to wait for her. The man who saved me got a medal for his bravery. I remember his name now – Mr Blackbeard. Luckily, my mother didn't punish me – maybe she thought that falling in the water would teach me not to disobey her again.

4 Decide if the following headlines would have been acceptable or not.

David's Story
Kind Teacher Becomes Strict Over Joke
Schoolboy Uses Frog To Play Trick On Teacher
Teacher Kills Frog After Schoolboy Joke
Teacher's Shirt Ruined By Ink

Gillie's Story
4 year-old Pushed Into Canal
Schoolgirl Attacked By Her Own Dog
Gillie Rescued By Factory Worker
Award For Man Who Rescued 4 year-old

5 Find words in Gillie's story which mean the following:

a man-made river
not permitted
very dirty
the noise a dog makes
fall down because of shock or illness

HOMEWORK

Write a story from your own childhood.

30 Looking Forward

1 Some science fiction writers were recently asked what their predictions were for the 21st Century. The article below is about what one person thinks life will be like.

Life in the 21st Century

As for daily life, I think that we will be able to order most of our shopping by computer and this will be delivered to our homes, so in fact there won't be any need to go out to the shops. I'm sure that most of our homes will have a video telephone so we will be able to see the person we are talking to. We will also be watching 'holovision' which will give you threedimensional life-size pictures on your screen – this will replace television. Because of improved technology, there will be no more road accidents. Cars will be guided by computers so people will not have to do any more driving.

I think most of our food will be in the form of pills and liquids which will have all the vitamins and protein that we need for a balanced diet. Only when we go out for social eating will we eat the same food as today, but we will no longer be eating meat.

About once a year our bodies will go into a health centre for a service in much the same way as a car has to be serviced. So, for example, our veins will be cleaned out, our blood purified, our muscles toned up and so on. Any part that is worn out could be replaced by a new plastic part. We will all be much healthier by then anyway, because there will be more leisure time for us to use for exercise. Also a safe medicine will have been discovered which will allow people to lose or put on weight as they need. One exciting development will be the possiblity of being deep frozen for a period of time and then waking up some years later. I would be interested in that myself!

A lot of our wildlife will be conserved in parks but unfortunately I think we will have lost the rhinoceros, the tiger and the panda and a few other species because of ruthless hunting by man. However, most of our energy problems will have been solved by developments in the use of solar energy and safe nuclear energy.

Because of improved media technology, all cultures will become similar and, indeed, everybody will be speaking an international language (English) by 2020.

There will be more women in politics than men – and the world will be a more peaceful place because of this. In fact, women will also be able to run the Marathon faster than men.

2 Write a list of the points you agree with and another list of the points you disagree with.

Agree	Disagree
Shopping by computer	Videophones in homes

3 Compare your list with other students. Explain your decisions.

4 Consider the following categories and write three predictions of your own for each one. Does the rest of the group accept your ideas?

Science and Technology
Sport
The Environment
Education
Health
The Home
Transport
Politics
Crime

5 In some parts of Britain people have buried Time Capsules which cannot be opened before 500 years have passed. In each Time Capsule they have put several objects which will give information about life in the 20th century that might be of interest to people in the future. Which five objects would you choose to put in a Time Capsule which would be opened in 500 years time?

6 **Balloon Debate**
You are in a balloon heading towards an undiscovered land. You have the chance to start a new civilization as you are the only survivors of the Third World War. In your balloon you have several inventions. If you don't keep them the technology will be lost and nobody will be able to reconstruct them. Unfortunately, the balloon is getting very heavy and you have to throw some of the inventions out. You are able to keep two inventions from the following list. Decide in groups which ones you want to keep and why.

petrol engine
anesthetic
television
watch
microchip computer
bicycle
fridge
X-ray machine

Teacher's Notes

UNIT 1 LIVING

LESSON 1 Around the World

1   Before the reading, set the scene by asking the students to brainstorm what they know about West Germany and the USA. As there is a specific task here, give the students a time limit in which they have to get as much information as possible to complete the charts.

3   Students can do this individually first and then compare their answers in pairs.

4   The students should be told that they will need their notes for the homework task. Show them how to make notes on the board. This is best done by using information from one of the students. For example, Sally: Rules *No smoking*.. As with all writing activities, you could to do the writing stage in class instead of for homework. This gives more opportunity to monitor the written work and give help and advice at the creative stage.

LESSON 2 Living at Home

1   Before doing this, ask students if they would like to have children, how many they would like, sons or daughters, etc. They could also be asked what the difficulties are of bringing up children. When asking each other questions, the students being asked should have their books closed so that they are forced to listen to the question rather than just reading from the book.

2   For **b** it is enough for students to write notes, for example, **(i)** *No make up*

3   Make sure that the students write their answers before they confer with each other. This will force them to defend their own opinion later on. Comparing answers could be done in pairs or in groups.

Homework: This should be displayed on classroom walls for further comparison.

LESSON 3 Another Country

1a This is best done in pairs as students can often get ideas from each other.

2b You could do a class poll here to see which is the most popular country overall. Get students to give reasons for their choices.

3   Students should do this individually and then compare their answers in pairs. Checking answers in pairs helps to create an atmosphere of mutual support and focuses on the student rather than the teacher. It can also save time if some mistakes are dealt with by the students themselves.

4   It may be necessary to show the students how to make notes, i.e. they are not expected to write out a whole sentence, but just one or two words.

Homework: It is a good idea to elicit some suggestions from the students before they are set the homework.

UNIT 2 THE POLICE AT WORK

LESSON 4 Missing People

1   Likely questions here will include the following:
   • When did you last see your husband?
   • What's his name?
   • How old is he?
   • Can you describe him?

3   It would be helpful to give students some information about the conventions of official forms in English, i.e. the use of **M** and **F** for male and female, and the meaning of Marital Status. Students will need to hear the tape more than once to fill in all the information.

4   Students will need to hear the section which contains the description of the man several times as there is a lot of information here.

LESSON 5 Accident

1   You could get the students to prepare questions for each other while looking at the picture. Alternatively, give the students one minute only to look at the picture and then organise a team competition, asking the questions yourself. A third possibility is to get the students to write the answers. This ensures greater participation but is more time consuming.

2   The meaning of these words can either be explained by pictures or by definition. When the students have completed this activity, point out that they have found the meaning of some completely unknown words just by reading the text. The skill of deducing the meaning of words from context is a very important one and students should be aware they have the skill to do it

4   This is best done in small groups. Students should be encouraged to make a list of the improvements they decide on for general feedback to the group.

5   Instead of this report students could be asked to write a report of the accident they were talking about in 3.

LESSON 6 Burglary

1   After a couple of minutes of pairwork you could write a list of the objects suggested by the students on the board. You could also draw on the experiences of the class by asking if anyone has had anything stolen from their house or car. This would provide a lead in to the next activity, and ask them to give their reasons.

7   Students may need to listen to the tape a number of times in order to get the details. However, it isn't necessary to insist on all the details here, just the ones the students can remember. It would be useful for them to compare their information in pairs before a final listening.

Homework: Students could discuss this in class before doing the written task.

UNIT 3 JOB

LESSON 7 Which Job?

1   This is a fluency activity that exploits the opinion gap. Give students time to think of the job they would like the most and the least and then explain their points of view to each other. Ask some students what they think at the end of the activity.

2   This should be done individually first, with students comparing answers in pairs afterwards.

LESSON 8 Applying for a Job

These texts are taken from *The Directory of Holiday Jobs Abroad*. Students might also be interested in *The Directory of Holiday Jobs in Britain* by Vacation Work Publications 9 Park End Street, Oxford OX1 1HJ.

4   This activity revises layout and conventions of formal letters in English.

LESSON 9 The Interview

1   Ask students if they have ever had an interview for a job. If there are students who have, then use this opportunity to find out what happened, what questions they were asked and how they felt. An additional activity which is useful here is to play the game 'What's my line' where one student thinks of a job and other students have to try to guess the job by asking yes/no questions. Usually the game is played with a limit on the number of questions that can be asked.

5   Students are not expected to write complete sentences here, but should complete the chart using notes as in the examples given.

UNIT 4 HOLIDAYS

LESSON 10 Going Places

1   The time limit should be observed, but it can be made into a group/pair competition to see who could get the most number of words in the time given.

6   This is an exercise in persuasion. Get students to make their choices individually first and then put them in groups of four to argue it out.

Homework: This could be organised as a competition. Students write their advertisements and then all the advertisements are displayed in the classroom. Students go around and choose which holiday they are most interested in.

LESSON 11 Ballooning

1   Make sure the students know the meaning of all the words before they put them in order. This should be done individually first and then in pairs/groups .

2   Students should be able to label the diagram by using the language surrounding the words in bold to deduce the meaning of these unknown words.

3   Explain that it is not necessary to read through the whole text. Students should scan the text for specific information. Give a time limit to encourage them to do this rather than read the text line by line.

LESSON 12 Complaining

1   This can simply be done by asking students outright. Alternatively, it can be done in pairs.

2   Some of the vocabulary in the advertisement may need explaining. You could pre-teach the following: *snooker, squash, fitness room, guides, inclusive*.

3   Only rough notes are expected from the students here. Once students have compared notes, the reasons for Mrs Wallis' complaints should be written on the board. This is essential, as without this information the students won't be able to do the guided writing activity.

UNIT 5 PEOPLE

LESSON 13 Choosing Partners

1   Students should do this activity in pairs/groups and compare answers.

2   For questions **a**, **b** and **c** the students should work individually to find their answers and then compare with each other. For the second part ask a few students for their opinions, but do not force students to contribute as it is a potentially embarrassing topic.

3   This is a fluency exercise, but to make it task based

students should be encouraged to write down definite answers for each question.

4 After this pair activity a class survey could be conducted to find out which are the most popular activities from the list (even if it is just a show of hands). Check to see if all the important hobbies and interests have been included.

Homework: Before setting this, revise the use of *have* + physical description and possessions and *be* + physical descriptions and qualities. For example,
My ideal partner should have blue eyes and dark hair.
My ideal partner should be tall and athletic.

LESSON 14 Judging People

2 There are no correct answers here, but students should be encouraged to discuss their opinions .

4 After the listening, tell the class who is who (see key) after checking students' opinions.

5 This may be a good opportunity to include the writing activity in class time so that students can attempt some group writing which can be monitored in class. The descriptions can be finished for homework and then the final product can be displayed for everyone to read and compare. Instead of the photos in the book, you could use some of your own photos and get the students to comment on these.

LESSON 15 Predicting Character

2 In **b** and **c** the students will need to listen to the tape several times.

3 You could point out that this sort of psychological test is designed to assess people's characters and is increasingly used in job interviews.

Homework: The final product should be displayed in the classroom so that all the students have the opportunity to read their horoscopes.

UNIT 6 SURVIVAL

LESSON 16 In the Antarctic

1 As an additional activity, get students to think of some other items that he probably took and to explain why. For example, *gun, mittens, boots, diary, sunglasses, compass,* etc.

4 To give speaking practice, this can be made a pair or group activity.

LESSON 17 Ky Ho

This lesson examines the story of a Vietnamese boat person. It might be helpful to explain some of the background to this story before starting the unit.

3 It is important to check the answers to the listening, otherwise the students will not be able to do the homework successfully. This should be done in some detail on the board.

LESSON 18 Castaway

1 Students should invent a story about how they got to the island either individually or in pairs. This could be told to the rest of the group. Students could use their story in the written task for homework.

3 To give students more speaking practice, this activity should be done in pairs.

4 The students should prepare this individually and then give their choices in groups. This could be prepared for homework, ready for discussion in the next lesson.

UNIT 7 HOUSE

LESSON 19 Renting a Room

2 It is important to get some feedback from students about their landlords and what rules they have insisted on.

3 Explain to students that they do not have to write full sentences when they are listening for information.

LESSON 20 A Place to Live

3 Students may need to listen to the tape several times to do the second part of this activity.

4 It is best to have a group of four for this activity: three householders and a buyer. The aim of this role play is to encourage fluency. Students should be allowed to see all the plans so that they can point out the deficiencies in each other's houses. The best procedure once the activity has been set up is for each householder to describe his/her house to the buyer in the group with the aim of selling it. Therefore only the good points should be mentioned. The buyer should ask any questions he/she wants, for example, *What about the railway line? How often do the trains go? Isn't it very noisy?* The other householders should be allowed to contradict these answers. It may be necessary to demonstrate this technique by doing a simple drawing on the board of, for example, a house by a motorway, and elicit the information that a possible advantage would be easy access to the motorway, but a disadvantage would be noise and air pollution caused by the traffic. The buyer must be forced into a decision; these are the only three houses on the market. Give a time limit for the buyer to choose and ask the buyer which one he/she chose and why.

LESSON 21 My Dream House

1 Give the students some time to make an individual choice before conducting a general feedback.

4 One way of doing this would be to give the students a nominal amount, i.e. £1 million, and ask them how much they would spend on each as a percentage.

5 Elicit some ideas before starting this activity. If there is time, some preparation in pairs or groups would help the weaker students. Display the final products.

UNIT 8 SPORT

LESSON 22 Training

1 Do this in pairs fairly quickly (five minutes) and then get some general feedback, especially on the advice given. Students should also be asked if they would take the advice.

3 Ask the students to write the answers and then compare them in pairs.

Homework: Some more artistic students may like to make their own poster using the framework given and draw their own illustrations.

LESSON 23 Getting Started

1 Get students to predict what Mike is going to say in pairs or groups. Listen to some suggestions.

2 Students should make notes as they listen to Mike's talk.

4 It may be helpful to pre-teach some of the verbs to help the students with the task, i.e. *raise, lean, stretch, rotate, swing.* This is best done by demonstration in the classroom.
You could get students to write their own exercise and ask other students to try to do the exercise by reading their instructions. Alternatively, the students could keep a record of their exercise schedule for a week. This could be discussed in a future lesson.

LESSON 24 Sumo Wrestling

2 Students should look for the answers individually and then compare their answers in pairs.

4 This could be organised as a group discussion or even a formal class debate after some group preparation. It is important to finish with a result, so a vote should be taken at the end of the debate.

UNIT 9 THE NATURAL WORLD

LESSON 25 Snakes

1 The students should be encouraged to guess here

and tell the rest of the class their predictions. This will motivate them to look for real answers in the text.

LESSON 26 World Problems

1 Today many people are 'green', or concerned about the environment. Ask students what they do to help preserve the environment.

2 The items given here will give you the chance to pre-teach some of the more complex vocabulary. Make sure the students understand them before they hear the talk. It is very important that the cartoons and the poems from the homework should be displayed.

LESSON 27 Zoo

1 Any answer is acceptable here provided that students can justify their choice.

2 This leads into **3** which can be done in pairs.

4 After listening to the argument for and against zoos, get the students to vote on whether they are for or against zoos in general.

UNIT 10 TIME

LESSON 28 Looking Back

1 Students should be encouraged to guess. As a follow up activity, ask the students to make up some questions of their own for a classroom quiz. This could involve the students in some active research - a possible homework task as an alternative to the one given.

2 Listen to some suggestions from the students. The aim here is get students to think what life was like 80 years ago and think about the difficulties in living in those times. This sets the scene for the listening in **3**.

4 There are no 'correct' answers to this question. The questions are designed to encourage the students to speculate on the woman's past which will give them the material to invent a story about her in the homework.

LESSON 29 Memories of Childhood

1 You may find that the best way to get this activity started is to tell a story from your own childhood and then elicit stories from any student who may be willing. This is quite a difficult activity, however, so some time may be needed for the students to prepare. Alternatively, this stage could be left until the end of the lesson when students could tell each other their stories in groups.

2 This should be taken as a light-hearted quiz, but students may prefer to do it individually. You could then get some feedback by asking individuals what score they got, without going into detail.

3 The students have to read for gist, so a time limit could be set here.

4 The students should be given longer for this activity as it requires a more intensive reading of the text. Make sure they can explain their answers.

Homework: Ideally a wall display could be made, so that students could read each other's stories.

LESSON 30 Looking Forward

1 If students are having difficulty extracting the information from this text, write these points on the board and get them to put them into two categories, AGREE and DISAGREE.
  • *shopping by computer*
  • *video telephone*
  • *'holovision'*
  • *no road accidents, etc*

4 Students write their own predictions (this could be done in pairs), read them out, and the rest of the group vote on whether they believe they will come true or not.

6 This activity is best done in groups. Students decide which ones they wish to keep and think of arguments they could use to convince the others. Again, a vote might be the best way to decide

Key

UNIT 1 LIVING

LESSON 1 Around the World

1	Anke Kirschbaum	Blythe Gardner
town	West Berlin	Lewistown
school	Gymnasium	Mixed sex high school
entertain-	Ballroom dancing	Watching TV
ment	Reading books	Reading books
	Writing letters	Cruising in cars
	Going to the cinema	
	Going to parties	
rules	Must be home by 10pm on weekdays	Must be home by 12.00

3a an only child pocket money nightlife confide (in) bilingual

b retired divorced receptionist profit licence

LESSON 2 Living at Home

2a Steph talked about the following:
her parents' age
being punished
smoking and drinking
her brother
the housework
her parents' love

(i) She was not allowed to wear make-up and she had to be back home by 10 o'clock.
(ii) She was sent to her room.
(iii) She had to do the housework.
(iv) They argued a lot and then got divorced.

LESSON 3 Another Country

2 *Possible answers*
new and unusual food
a different climate
having to make new friends
finding somewhere to live
new customs and habits
missing your home country

3a for work, for his job
b springtime, gardens, parks, friendliness of the people, quality of life, theatres, concerts, musicals (cultural life), roast beef.
c (climbing in) the mountains

4	likes	dislikes
	Cambridge	It's difficult to make
	rhythm of life	friends
	people respect	the food
	privacy/independence	the weather
	beautiful countryside	

5a to learn the language and meet the people
b 1969
c the good weather

UNIT 2 THE POLICE AT WORK

LESSON 4 Missing People

3a **a** hair **b** forehead **c** eyebrow **d** cheek **e** moustache **f** beard **g** jacket **h** tie **i** shirt **j** neck **k** lips **l** glasses

3 **Name** James Freeman
Age 47
Sex M
Marital Status Married
Address The Cedars, Highworth Avenue, Manchester

Telephone Manchester 21600
Physical Features Round face, beard, moustache, going bald (not much hair), dark bushy eyebrows
Last seen:
Time In the morning
Place Station
Clothes Suit, blue shirt, tie
Additional Information:

4 The missing man is **F**.

5 The wanted man is **C**.

LESSON 6 Burglary

4 1, 2, 4, and 6 are answered by Mrs Taylor.
7 **Stolen items:**
1 Ferguson video (C)
2 silver bracelet, three inches thick, plain chain connecting it (B)
3 two blue Chinese vases (H)
4 Olympus 10 camera (I)
5 pair of binoculars, Zanussi (J)
6 pair of large silver candlesticks, matching pair; Victorian (F)
7 large black leather suitcase, initialled DG (D)

UNIT 3 JOB

LESSON 7 Which Job?

3 **age:** 20–28
height: 5ft. 4 or 1m 62
other requirements:
a good standard of education
must have a 10 year British or EEC (European Economic Community) passport
good health
good eyesight (no glasses allowed but contact lenses OK)
able to swim 25 metres
able to reach Gatwick airport within 1 hour and 15 minutes

4	Paragraph 1	Introducing Debbie Mason
	Paragraph 2	Getting the Job
	Paragraph 3	Training
	Paragraph 4	The Route and my Job
	Paragraph 5	Health Problems
	Paragraph 6	Working Hours
	Paragraph 7	Social Life and Family Life

5a True
b False: serving food only takes 10% of her time
c True
d False: She has more free time than in most other full-time jobs
e True
f False: She sees her boyfriend often because they work together

LESSON 8 Applying for a Job

1 **a** 4 **b** 3 **c** 2 **d** 3 **e** 1 **f** 2 **g** 1 **h** 4

2a 3 Grape picking in France
b 4 Work camp in Morocco
c 2 Chambermaid in Germany
d 2 Chambermaid in Germany
3a Because she needs to earn some money and the Moroccan job isn't paid.
b Because the cost of living is high and it is very expensive here.

c It goes on too long and she doesn't speak the languages required.

4a (vi) **b** (i) **c** (iv) **d** (iii) **e** (ii) **f** (v)

LESSON 9 The Interview

3 **Do** arrive on time.
Don't smoke during the interview
Do wear smart clothes.
Don't worry about being nervous
Do be polite
Do express your own opinions
Do find out about the company before you go
Do prepare your questions
Do find out the name of the person who is going to interview you
Do be confident

5		First applicant	Second applicant
	name	Beth Gordon	Annie West
	age	23	25
	nationality	British	British
	previous experience	Worked at a university	Worked in a youth club
	additional information	Driving licence Speaks French and Spanish	Driving licence Has driven a minibus Interest in sport Has been to France and Spain

UNIT 4 HOLIDAYS

LESSON 10 Going Places

2 The following are important:
good weather
cheap prices
interesting food
sports facilities
3a last year
b nine months
c two girl friends
d friendly people and felt safe
e five months
f waitressing and selling over the phone
g English accents

5	A	camping	G	pot holing
	B	sailing	H	painting
	C	horse riding	I	windsurfing
	D	climbing	J	wine tasting
	E	pottery	K	hang gliding
	F	archery	L	canoeing

LESSON 11 Ballooning

2a gas cylinder **b** fire extinguisher **c** trailing rope **d** carrying handles **e** basket **f** burner **g** mouth **h** cooling vent **i** envelope
3a In the morning or evening
b 5.30
c five
d 1 hour
e 2 000 feet
f By car – it follows the balloon

LESSON 12 Complaining

3 Mrs Wallis complains of the following:
No minibus at the station
It is not explained in the brochure that dogs are not allowed

There was only one tennis court and this was always booked
Hospitable family – away on holiday
There weren't any guides

UNIT 5 PEOPLE

LESSON 13 Choosing Partners

2a Dateline
b It finds partners for people
c Complete the coupon for the guide (address given at the bottom of the advertisement)

LESSON 14 Judging People

1a (viii) **b** (vi) **c** (v) **d** (ii) **e** (ix) **f** (i) **g** (iii) **h** (iv) **i** (vii) **j** (x)
4 A Monica   C Julian
   B Mick   D Cintia

LESSON 15 Predicting Character

1 A reading palms
   B reading cards
   C analysing blood groups
   D studying people's handwriting
   E studying the position of stars when people were born
   F studying the shape of people's bodies

2a She is reading Simon's palm.
b interested in ideas, serious, kind, generous, likeable
c will travel
   will meet his wife when he is 32
   will have three children
   will have good health and will live into his eighties or nineties
   will have a lot of money

UNIT 6 SURVIVAL

LESSON 16 In the Antarctic

1a stove **b** anorak **c** sledge **d** skis **e** tent **f** sleeping bag **g** rucksack
2a hot chocolate, biscuits, butter, oatmeal blocks, hot drink, soup, salami, tea
b 5,100 calories
c Tea doesn't give any calories and tea-bags are heavy to carry
d 16 kilometres per day
e 160 kilos

3 He complains of the following:
   thirst – line 4
   hunger – lines 9–10
   pain – line 16 and line 20
   boredom – line 5
   tiredness – line 14

LESSON 17 Ky Ho

1a Vietnam
b five years ago
c by writing to the Prime Minister, the Home Office and the Vietnamese government
d Millfield
e mathematics and science
f to follow a career in computers and electronics
g canoe building and sailing

2a (iii) **b** (vi) **c** (v) **d** (i) **e** (ii) **f** (iv)
4 **Date of departure from Vietnam** 27 Sep. 1978
   Reasons for his escape To get away from the war in Vietnam and avoid doing military service
   Details of the boat 50 feet long, 162 people (very crowded), only fruit and biscuits to eat, many people seasick
   Details of life on the island Terrible, no fresh water, no fruit, people living in huts
   Date of arrival in Britain July 1979

LESSON 18 Castaway

2a palm tree **b** stream **c** rocks **d** mountain **e** sea **f** raft **g** hut **h** well **i** canoe **j** bush **k** beach **l** cave **m** wave
5 Ted Zapp chooses the following:
   cassette Abbey Road – The Beatles
   book A collection of science fiction stories
   useful object Swiss army knife
   luxury item a guitar
   animal monkey

UNIT 7 HOUSE

LESSON 19 Renting a Room

3 The landlord says the following things: **The bathroom** – Can bath once a day, at any time. **The kitchen** – Can use at any time before 8.00 am and after 7.30 pm. **Having parties** – OK, but not too often. Finish by twelve. Tell the landlord in advance.
The telephone – Put the money for the calls in the black box. No incoming calls after 11 o'clock. **Smoking** – Not allowed.
Music and television – Not after 11.30 pm. **Towels, sheets and blankets** – Bring your own towels. Sheets and blankets provided.
4 The differences are:
The landlord now says that it is forbidden to watch TV after 10.30 – before he said 11.30
He now says the bath is to be taken between 6.00 and 8.00 pm. – before he said at no particular time
He now says no parties are allowed – before he said some parties were allowed as long as you tell the landlord
He now says you may receive incoming calls only – before he said that outgoing calls could be made and money for the calls should be placed in a box provided
He now says you must bring sheets and towels – before he said that sheets would be provided

LESSON 20 A Place to Live

2a hall **b** sitting-room **c** study **d** patio **e** garden **f** kitchen **g** bathroom **h** second bedroom **i** main bedroom **j** bedroom/storeroom
3 The agent mentions the following: a large garden, central heating, in a quiet area, thick solid walls, large bathroom, near good schools

LESSON 21 My Dream House

3a 1971
b 8 bedrooms
c one – a gardener
d a teacher (of woodwork)
e it made him ill
f he runs a furniture factory
g an aeroplane

UNIT 8 SPORT

LESSON 22 Training

2 No real answer to this but a recent article came up with the following order for overall fitness: swimming, basketball, badminton, running, football, tennis, gymnastics, weightlifting, golf.

3 1 490 BC
   2 Greece
   3 One of the cities
   4 42 kilometres
   5 2 hours 8 minutes

4 **a** 3 months
   b 80 kilometres
   c 30 kilometres
   d Yes
   e Keep warm and drink a lot
   f Jog for a short distance

Homework
Training
1 Start training three months before the start of a race.
2 Eat a balanced diet including a lot of carbohydrates.
3 Run 80 kilometres in the early days – add more later.
4 Do loosening up exercises before you start running.
Race Day
1 Eat your breakfast at least three hours before the start of the race.
2 Drink a lot of water half an hour before the race.
3 Drink water during the race and sponge yourself with water if it is very hot.
After the Race
1 Keep moving after the race.
2 Drink a lot in the two or three hours after the race.

LESSON 23 Getting Started

2 Distance: Start slowly – build up to more later
Clothes and Shoes: Buy good shoes but don't worry about clothes
Getting Ready: Warm up before you start running
Eating: Don't eat for at least two hours before the start of a run
Benefits of running: Very relaxing
3a head **b** neck **c** shoulder **d** trunk **e** hip **f** thigh **g** knee **h** calf **i** heel **j** ankle **k** sole
4 1 E 2 F 3 A 4 C 5 D 6 B 7 G

LESSON 24 Sumo Wrestling

2a 15 days
b A few seconds
c They don't now. They used to hundreds of years ago.
d To attract the gods.
e To allow food and drink to turn to fat.
f 12 to 13.
3 *basho* a tournament lasting 15 days
dohyo the ring where the fight takes place
mawashi a belt, make of silk, worn by the wrestler
chankonabe a dish of meat or fish with vegetables
yokozuna a grand champion

UNIT 9 THE NATURAL WORLD

LESSON 25 Snakes

1a 12 kilometres per hour
b 13 metres
c rats, mice, frogs, birds, lizards and fish
d India
e Possible answers: adder; viper; krait, rattlesnake, cobra, sea-snakes, coral snakes etc
f Python, Boa constrictor etc.
g Yes, once in Burma and once in Mozambique
3a Boa constrictor, Python and Rattlesnake
b to be kept warm
   plenty of water
   a small enclosure
   food twice a week
c rats, mice and other rodents
d £50–£80
4a The order of instructions is as follows:
   Warm the person.
   Remove wet clothing and dry the person.
   Give warm food and drink.
   Don't give any alcohol.
   Consult a doctor if the condition appears serious.
b The following advice is given for snake bites:
   Keep person relaxed

Wash area of the bite in water.
Keep part of body bitten off the ground.
Seek medical help for young children.

LESSON 26 World Problems

2a Dr Lawton mentions the following:
saving energy
recycling glass and paper
joining an action group
the ozone layer
using lead free petrol
buying organic food

b **(i)** use a bike instead of a car
turn off the lights in your house when
they are not in use
use the minimum temperature when
cooking
reduce the temperature of your house
by 5 degrees

(ii) it's better for the environment
it's cheaper

(iii) Greenpeace
Friends of the Earth

LESSON 27 Zoo

1 *Possible answers*
giraffe – is not a member of the cat family
dog – the only one normally kept as a pet
rat – the only one whose meat is not normally
eaten
bear – the only one not used to transport people
monkey – the others are all threatened with
extinction

5a The two main aims are to protect animals with
a breeding programme and to educate the
public.

b Her father.

c Panda, tiger and rhinoceros.

d Jewellery (from ivory), ashtrays (from gorilla's
feet) and also animal furs are mentioned.

e Food for the animals, enclosures for the
animals, staff salaries, electricity, facilities for the
public, vets' bills and repairs to buildings are
mentioned.

LESSON 28 Looking Back

1 1 1901 2 1825 3 1953 4 1961 5 1876
6 1885 7 1840's

3a False: she had her own room although it was
very small

b True

c True

d False: they didn't have central heating, but the
Bodley in the kitchen kept the house warm.

e False: they didn't have fridges then.

f True

g True
Things she did with her free time include:
playing games, reading, knitting and playing on
the beach.

LESSON 29 Memories of Childhood

3a Keith **b** Annie **c** Gillie **d** David

Tapescripts

LESSON 2 ACTIVITY 2a

INTERVIEWER Steph, now that you're starting
your college ... erm you've left home for the first
time ... looking back, what do you think about the
way your parents brought you up?

STEPH Well I think on the whole I had an excellent
upbringing ... erm ... I think my parents
understood me very well erm ... If they hadn't
understood me quite so well I think things could
have gone very badly wrong ... erm ... my parents
were different in that they were considerably older
than most people's ... erm ... my mother was forty
five when she had me ... erm ... I was also the last
of six and in that position I always felt very secure
... there was never any doubt that my parents
loved me and ... erm ... that was a ... a good thing
. Erm ... there were also very few rules in our
house. They never said to me ... you know, 'you
must be home at a certain time' and ... erm ...
'you must do this' and 'you must do that'. I used to
come home when I wanted and that trust I think
made me very very responsible, certainly more
responsible than most people of my age. Erm ...
again, they never said to me, you know, 'You ...
you mustn't drink and you mustn't smoke.' Erm ...
I also could always talk to my parents about
things and argue with them. Erm ... the only time
that I remember that my father and parents got
very angry with me was once when I got very
drunk . My father hit me, but ... erm ... because
he was worried, and the next morning he made
me get up and go to school, which again, I think
instilled a lot of responsibility that you can do
things but you have to be more responsible for
them than most people realise. Erm ... one of the
only criticisms I can make is that ... erm ... they
never made me do enough housework, the result
of which is that I can't cook now and I think they
should have pushed me more in that ... that
direction. Erm ... having said I didn't do very
much housework, they made my brother do even

less which made me feel a bit jealous of him
because I think felt he got away with more than
me. Erm ... er ... with regard to my academic
career as well, I always felt a bit jealous of that,
because they consulted him more and talked
about ... about it more with him, whereas with
me they just let me get on with it and I felt that
they took my ... erm ... future less seriously than
they did, but ... erm ... maybe that's so, maybe
not.

LESSON 2 ACTIVITY 2b

INTERVIEWER Rudi, can you tell me ... erm ...
about your parents and the way they brought you
up?

RUDI Yes ... erm ... we were given a lot of freedom
or quite a lot of freedom, my brother and I... . erm
... although I was not allowed to wear make up ...
my father didn't like that, and ... erm ... I had to
be in in the evening by ten o'clock. Erm ... if
anything ever went wrong at home if we were
naughty, then we were sent to our rooms usually,
but er ... there was nothing worse than that. Er ...
we were usually quite good. Erm ... pocket
money: I was given pocket money every Thursday,
but this was in exchange for housework such as
washing up, hoovering the house or cooking ...
something I enjoyed doing, though. Erm ... I also
think that my brother and I were treated equally.
We were both given the same amounts of money
and given the same freedom, and all in all I think
that ... erm ... we were brought up quite
successfully. Erm, there is one er, negative point,
maybe. My father and mother argued quite a lot
and erm ... they've just got divorced, so this was a
problem at home, but my brother and I were
given a lot of freedom and enjoyed living at home.

LESSON 3 ACTIVITY 4

INTERVIEWER Theresa, which country are you
from?

THERESA I'm from Spain.

INTERVIEWER And when and why did you come
to live in England?

THERESA Oh, I came – this was a long time ago – I
came in '69 for the first time. I was then a student
... erm ... at home in Spain. I was studying
English, so I thought it'd be a good idea to come
to this country to practise the language, and
become acquainted with the people.

INTERVIEWER And now you speak English
perfectly and you're still here. What do you like
about living in England?

THERESA Erm ... well, it's very difficult I think ...
erm ... to say. I, well, I like the place where I live
which is Cambridge. Erm ... I like the pace, the
rhythm of life, I think. I am now more used to this
timetable, so to speak ... er, different, er, from
what it is at home. Erm ... I like also the way they
respect your privacy ... er ... your independence
... erm, what else? Erm ... I don't know, the
countryside, but of course erm ... when it comes
... when summer comes er, and it begins to rain,
perhaps it spoils the whole thing, but it's very
beautiful to look at. It's ... it's rather like a
beautiful picture.

INTERVIEWER And what do you dislike about
living in England?

THERESA Erm ... Well I suppose one of the
difficulties in this country is to make friends. And
... and also, living in Cambridge, there is always
the temptation of ... er, joining with the foreign
crowd, with the foreigners, even with people of
the same nationality as er ... yourself, and, erm ...
well, I can imagine it may ... maybe in the long
run it may become rather lonely perhaps, but I
still ... I haven't suffered from that er ... difficulty
yet.

INTERVIEWER So what advice would you give to
somebody coming to live in England?

THERESA Oh, come with an open mind. Er, do not
... erm ... compare all the time and say, 'oh, at
home things are like this or like that', but rather
try to understand perhaps and adapt and try to

make … make the most of it while you're here.

INTERVIEWER What do you miss about Spain?

THERESA Er, nothing much, because I go quite often, but I suppose erm … this reference I made to the weather before … er … perhaps the weather, even though it's rather topical – one always complains about the weather in this country – but it can get you down I think, in the long run. Yes month after month say, of dull, misty, humid weather. Otherwise, well, it's precisely what I … it's rather paradoxical … it's precisely what you don't like about er … what you do like about England and the English people – the fact that they respect your privacy and leave you alone – it can go to extremes and then it becomes, as I say, indifference, and … erm … that's precisely what we don't have at home. It's exactly the opposite. At home everyone interferes with your life. People are nosey and they all want to know what you're doing, perhaps with very good intentions, but then it becomes too much and it is interference. And … and I dislike that, anyway, because I've seen that there are other possibilities.

INTERVIEWER A lot of foreigners complain about English food. How does that strike you?

THERESA Yes, well I agree with that, yes … erm, but I live on my own so I don't have to suffer it in a sense, I … I can cook myself or I can … er … get round it and also I think in fact … er it has influenced me … er to such an extent that I don't care much now about food. So, yes I must say, for someone who er … comes er …to this country for the first time it is a bit of a shock. There's no doubt about it.

INTERVIEWER Do you think you'll continue to live in England or would you like to go back to Spain?

THERESA I think I will continue to stay, yes, at least for a few years, yes.

UNIT 2

LESSON 4 ACTIVITY 3

POLICEMAN Hello, Trafford Police Station.

WOMAN Erm … he … hello. I wonder if you can help me … erm my husband hasn't come home.

POLICEMAN I see, Madam. And erm … can I have your name please?

WOMAN It's Mrs Freeman.

POLICEMAN Mrs Freeman … And, er, your address?

WOMAN The Cedars …

POLICEMAN … The Cedars …

WOMAN … that's C–E–D–A–R–S …

POLICEMAN … C–E–D–A–R–S , yes …

WOMAN Highworth Avenue, that's H–I–G–H–W–O–R–T–H

POLICEMAN … Highworth Avenue …

WOMAN … Manchester.

POLICEMAN Manchester. And the telephone number?

WOMAN Er 21600.

POLICEMAN Right, and er … when did you last see him, madam?

WOMAN Er, well, it must have been … eight o'clock … I … I drove him to the station to catch the train and … he's due home at six, you see and … it's now after midnight and … well, I'm very worried because I mean … he always would telephone me if there was any problem, so I don't know what to do

POLICEMAN … no, I see. Erm … right, can you give me a few details about him er … what's his name, Madam?

WOMAN James Freeman.

POLICEMAN James Freeman, yes …

WOMAN Er … and … and he's forty seven years old.

POLICEMAN Forty seven, right … for ty seven. And … erm … what … can you give me a physical description … how tall he is … er …

WOMAN Yes, he's about … er, he's five foot eleven.

POLICEMAN Five feet eleven, yes …

WOMAN … and, erm … he's bearded …

POLICEMAN … bearded

WOMAN … and he's got a moustache. Erm … and he's … he's sort of sandy coloured hair.

POLICEMAN Right.

WOMAN Er … I'd say his face was a sort of square face really, and he's got quite heavy … um … eyebrows.

POLICEMAN Right. That's … that's fine. Er … is he wearing glasses at all?

WOMAN No, no, he doesn't wear glasses.

POLICEMAN Right … er … and, er … can you remember what he was wearing?

WOMAN Well, he was wearing his dark suit, that's his… his dark navy blue suit and …

POLICEMAN … suit …

WOMAN … and, er …

POLICEMAN … and a tie, of course, I suppose …

WOMAN Yes, that's right. It was a … a dark blue tie with very small white spots on it.

POLICEMAN Right … oh that's very good.

WOMAN And a blue shirt …

POLICEMAN Yes … All right now, so it's er, it's Mr James Freeman.

WOMAN That's right …

POLICEMAN Erm … er … age forty seven, height five feet eleven …

WOMAN Yes.

POLICEMAN … dark blue suit … you … er … you haven't seen him since eight o'clock this morning and he should have been home by six, is that right?

WOMAN … that's right. That's quite correct.

POLICEMAN Er … well, it's a bit early to er … to do anything just at the moment …

WOMAN I see …

POLICEMAN Er … what I'm going to ask you to do, Madam, is if you could ring tomorrow, if there's still no news, and erm … after that time he will be registered as a missing person.

WOMAN I see … so I … I … I can… I can ring you tomorrow to find out if you've got any news, you see …

POLICEMAN Yes … I mean, er I'm sure there's er you know, there's some very normal explanation for this, there … … very … usually is er, in these cases.

WOMAN I see.

POLICEMAN Not … er, you mustn't worry. I'm sure it'll be all right.

WOMAN Right, well, that's very kind of you and I … I certainly will ring you … you don't mind how early I ring …?

POLICEMAN No, not at all, not at all.

WOMAN I see. Well, thank you, you've been very kind.

POLICEMAN That's … that's all right Madam,

goodbye.

WOMAN Goodbye, goodbye.

LESSON 5 ACTIVITY 5

KATE Fulham police station. Can I help you?

MRS TAYLOR Yes, er … erm look I don't … I don't know if I'm doing the right thing, but I've just seen two men come out of the house opposite me … carrying a rather large suitcase and I know the Greens, who live at the house, they're away at the moment. Well, I wasn't sure if I should phone you or not, but … well, you see I'm not that sort of person the one …

KATE No, no, no … that's quite all right. It's … er better to be safe than sorry isn't it? Now, do you think you could give me your name and address?

MRS TAYLOR Yes, it's … it's Mrs Taylor … and I live at number 23 Finlay Street. That's, er is just off the Fulham Palace Road.

KATE … 23 … Finlay Street … right. Now … erm … you said you saw two men come out of the house opposite you?

MRS TAYLOR Yes, that's right, and then they got into a white van and … and … and they drove off …

KATE Can you tell me … What's the number of the house they came out of?

MRS TAYLOR Number 24. It's the house where the Greens live.

KATE Right. And can you give me a description of the two men?

MRS TAYLOR No, I … I'm afraid I can't. I didn't get a very good look at them to tell the truth …

KATE No? Oh, well … erm … could you describe the van please?

MRS TAYLOR Er well, I can't say very much about it … well … it was definitely white. It was large, and it drove off in the direction of the river.

KATE Erm … did you get the number plate of the van, madam?

MRS TAYLOR No … no, I'm afraid I didn't.

KATE Well how long ago did this happen?

MRS TAYLOR Oh just a couple of minutes ago … I … I thought I should phone you straight away.

KATE Right, well … co … could you hold the line please, Mrs Taylor – I'm just going to radio our patrol cars so that they can keep a look out, and then I'll get back to you … is that OK?

MRS TAYLOR Yeah, OK … right.

LESSON 6 ACTIVITY 6

POLICEMAN Right, if I can just take a few details of what you've had stolen … what seems to be missing …

MR GREEN Yes … of course, of course … er … I have them written here, actually.

POLICEMAN Right

MR GREEN Er … there's a Ferguson video

POLICEMAN Ferguson …

MR GREEN Yes …

POLICEMAN Erm … does that have a serial number?

MR GREEN No, I'm afraid not I … I … I … I meant to jot it down but I haven't … haven't … didn't do so in fact. Er … erm … a silver bracelet.

POLICEMAN This would be your wife's bracelet.

MR GREEN Yes er … er … about … erm, I suppose, three inches in … in, erm, thickness … just a round, plain …

POLICEMAN ... yes ... plain ...

MR GREEN ... with a kind of chain ... when you open it there's a ... there's a chain connecting it ...

POLICEMAN ... got the picture, yes ...

MR GREEN ... er ... made in France ...

POLICEMAN ... would that have a ...

MR GREEN It has got 'Made in France' on it.

POLICEMAN But no kind of hallmark or anything you ...

MR GREEN No ... no ...

POLICEMAN ... could have jotted down.

MR GREEN And two blue Chinese vases ... excuse me ... erm ...

POLICEMAN Would they be large?

MR GREEN Yeah ... well, they're about eight ... eight inches, I suppose ...

POLICEMAN ... eight inches ...

MR GREEN ... and they're matching ... erm ...

POLICEMAN Yes. What sort of blue?

MR GREEN It's a kind of mixture. It goes from a ... a dark, dark ... erm ... navy blue er ... into a lighter blue.

POLICEMAN Oh right, oh it's a willow pattern type thing.

MR GREEN No ... it's ... it's ... it's a sort of one colour kind of fading out into another ... do you know?

POLICEMAN Yup.

MR GREEN Erm ... an Olympus OM10 camera.

POLICEMAN OM10

MR GREEN OM10 ... that's the ... that's the ... the ... you know, erm ...

POLICEMAN ... the model ... the model ... the model number.

MR GREEN The model, exactly.

POLICEMAN Got it. OM10 ... just one moment. Got that. Yes?

MR GREEN Erm ... a pair of, er, binoculars ... er ...made by Zanussi ...

POLICEMAN Zanussi ...

MR GREEN Zanussi, yes ...

POLICEMAN Are they Japanese or are they Italian? I can never remember.

MR GREEN Yes ...

POLICEMAN Now ... how do you spell ... just ... Zanussi?

MR GREEN Oh ... Zanussi ... that's er ... Z–A–N

POLICEMAN Z–A–N ...

MR GREEN U double S I

POLICEMAN U double S I, got it, yes ...

MR GREEN Yes ...erm, a pair of large er silver candlesticks. Er ... I suppose ... they're about a foot, actually, they're very large.

POLICEMAN Would they be ... branch?

MR GREEN No, no they're ... they're two separate candlesticks, a matching pair.

POLICEMAN Right

MR GREEN I'm afraid again, no serial num ... no hallmark or anything on these, but ...

POLICEMAN How old would they be?

MR GREEN Oh they're Victorian.

POLICEMAN Victorian.

MR GREEN Yes.

POLICEMAN Right. OK ...

MR GREEN And er ... a ... a ... a large black suit case, leath ... leather suitcase

POLICEMAN ... which presumably ...

MR GREEN ... which they took everything away in ... yeah ...

POLICEMAN That's the way, they've got cheek, haven't they ...

MR GREEN Well, yes, well ...

POLICEMAN Er...any identifying marks on the suitcase?

MR GREEN Er, yes, it's got two straps which go ... go round it ... if that's an identifying mark, is it?

POLICEMAN. Yes.

MR GREEN. Oh, it's ... it's ... it's initialled. Erm ... erm ... DG

POLICEMAN. OK. DG. And that's ... that's all as far as you can remember at this moment.

MR GREEN. That's ... that's all, yes ...

POLICEMAN. Right. Thank you very much indeed.

UNIT 3

LESSON 7 ACTIVITY 3

RECRUITMENT OFFICER. Virgin Atlantic Staff Recruitment, can I help you?

MARK. Yes, good morning ... erm I'm interested in applying for a job as one of your cabin staff, and I wondered if you could tell me your requirements.

RECRUITMENT OFFICER. Certainly. Well, first of all age ... you've got to be between twenty and twenty eight, unless of course you've flown with another airline ...

MARK. No, no, I haven't done that.

RECRUITMENT OFFICER. Ah, well the maximum age is twenty eight then. The minimum height is five foot four inches or one metre sixty two. You've got to have a good standard of education; you must hold a ten year British or EEC passport, and you must, of course, be in good physical health ... oh ... you can't wear glasses, though.

MARK Oh, I see ... er, well, I don't actually wear glasses, but I do wear contact lenses ...

RECRUITMENT OFFICER. Oh, contact lenses are fine. That's no problem. You must be able to swim a minimum of 25 metres and, finally, you've got to be able to get to Gatwick within about an hour and fifteen minutes for stand–by duties.

MARK. Oh, I see, oh that's all right. I live in Sevenoaks – that's fine, isn't it?

RECRUITMENT OFFICER. Oh yes, that's plenty close enough ... OK ... are you still interested?

MARK. Yes, I am ... erm ... I wonder if you could send me your application form and some information about salary, conditions, training and so on?

RECRUITMENT OFFICER. Yes, of course ... well, I'll send out details with the application form. Could I have your name and address please?

MARK. My name's Stevenson.

RECRUITMENT OFFICER. Stevenson ... and your initial?

MARK. ... is M.

RECRUITMENT OFFICER. Right ... M. Stevenson.

MARK. And my address is 59 ... Elm Avenue ...

RECRUITMENT OFFICER. 59 Elm Avenue.

MARK. Sevenoaks ...

RECRUITMENT OFFICER. Sevenoaks. And the postcode?

MARK. Oh, I'm afraid I don't know that.

RECRUITMENT OFFICER. Well, never mind. I'll put it in the post today.

MARK. Thank you very much – goodbye.

LESSON 8 ACTIVITY 2

JUDITH. Hello Sharon

SHARON. Hi Judith

JUDITH. Well, what did you think of those job advertisements I sent you?

SHARON. Well, they weren't bad. I quite ... er ... I quite liked the one in France. But the problem there is I've got to be back in England by September 20th, I've got a wedding to go to.

JUDITH. Oh

SHARON. I ... I quite liked the one in Morocco as well. I'd quite like to do some ... er ... social welfare work.

JUDITH. Yes, I know, but I've got a problem about that, 'cause I need to earn some money ... and that one's unpaid, isn't it

SHARON. Yeah, that one is. Yeah, that one's definitely unpaid

JUDITH. What about the one in Germany? The money's really good and we'd get our weekends free

SHARON. Yeah, yeah. Yeah, it sounds good. The only thing with that one, when I looked at it, was ... er ... let me check, yeah. Yeah, there's no accomodation included. And the cost of living's quite high in Germany. I've been there before it's ...

JUDITH. ... is it?

SHARON. ... really high, what about Italy? What do you reckon there?

JUDITH. Yeah. I mean, I'd love to go to Italy, but ... oh, hang on ... no, I can't, because it says you've got to speak ... German, Italian or French. I ... I don't speak any of those. I think the one in Munich was going to suit us best really, you know.

SHARON. Yeah, I quite like Munich. I've been there before with my parents ...

JUDITH. Is it nice?

SHARON. Yeah, it is really good. But er ... oh, I don't know if I really fancy working as a chambermaid.

JUDITH. Oh, it's only for a few months. It'd be really good experience for us.

SHARON. Oh, I know. I mean, the money would be good ...

JUDITH. Yeah.

SHARON. Oh, all right. Let's go for that one.

JUDITH. Great.

SHARON. Are you going to write to them?

JUDITH. Yeah, I'll write.

SHARON. All right.

LESSON 9 ACTIVITY 5

First Applicant

INTERVIEWER. Er ... good morning.

BETH. Hello.

INTERVIEWER. Now, can I just check one or two details? You're Beth Gordon..

BETH. Yes ... that's right.

INTERVIEWER. And you're twenty three.

BETH. mm

INTERVIEWER. ... and you were born in England?

BETH. Yes, yes, I was.

INTERVIEWER. Yes, so English is your mother tongue?

BETH. Yes, that's right, yes.

INTERVIEWER.OK, erm … so can you tell me of any experience you've, had in a similar job before?

BETH.Well, I … I've only just graduated, as you'll see from my CV, but I have had a lot of experience at university with the … the type of … you know, sort of social activities that you have at the college … Erm, for example, I … I was involved in lots of societies … erm … where I have to organise things for oh, a lot of students together and … er … I … I think it's quite similar to the type of things you be organising at the college.

INTERVIEWER.I see, so you've had some experience and … and you enjoyed the work did you?

BETH.Oh yeah, yeah, I loved it … I like being with people.

INTERVIEWER.Mm… erm … can you speak any languages?

BETH.Er yes I can speak Spanish and French fluently, because that was my degree.

INTERVIEWER.Oh, you did both Spanish and French?

BETH.Yeah, I did a joint honours degree.

INTERVIEWER.Fine and … erm … have you got a driving licence?

BETH.Yes I have … I've had it since I was seventeen.

INTERVIEWER.And can you drive the minibus?

BETH.Erm … I can't, no, but I'm willing to have a go.

INTERVIEWER.Right, I see. Erm … now, this is initially for a six month period, but would you be interested in continuing if we wanted you to?

BETH.Well, actually, I'd like to have the job for six months because I want to save up some money to go travelling again. But, you know, it … it depends … if I really enjoyed it and got settled in, then perhaps, well you know … I … I'd er consider staying on for a longer period of time.

INTERVIEWER.Mm … and why do you think you'd be good at this job?

BETH.Well … er … I … I've travelled before in my holidays from university … I've been to several different countries and I like being with foreign people. I like meeting people and I enjoy generally the type of things that I'd be required to do in the job … and I … I just like being with people, I guess.

INTERVIEWER.Fine … OK … well, if you'd like to go with Roger he'll show you around the college and you can ask him any questions and then perhaps we can have another little chat when you've had your visit.

BETH.OK … thanks very much.

INTERVIEWER.Right. Thank you very much for coming.

BETH.Thank you.

Second Applicant

INTERVIEWER.Good morning.

ANNIE.Good morning.

INTERVIEWER.Now, you must be Annie West – is that right?

ANNIE.That's right, yeah.

INTERVIEWER.OK, and English is your mother tongue?

ANNIE.That's right.

INTERVIEWER.Yeah, that's fine … and you're twenty five?

ANNIE.Yes.

INTERVIEWER.Great. Annie, have you had much experience of this sort of work before?

ANNIE.No … well, I've worked in a youth club – a local club – for about three years helping organise events and mainly doing DJ work at the weekends at the discos.

INTERVIEWER.Is that fairly recently?

ANNI. Oh yeah, yeah.

INTERVIEWER.And you enjoyed that, did you?

ANNIE.Yes, I really enjoyed that. I like music.

INTERVIEWER.Mm … erm … I see you've been to Southampton Polytechnic … did you get involved in many social activities there?

ANNIE.Not on the organising side, I was a member of the volleyball team …

INTERVIEWER.So you're quite interested in sport.

ANNIE Yeah, I like sport, yeah.

INTERVIEWER.OK … er … have you ever been abroad?

ANNIE.Yes I have. I've been to France and I've been to Spain.

INTERVIEWER.Mm … and have you worked with foreign people?

ANNIE.No I haven't … erm … not at all. I went on an exchange visit from school to France when I was sixteen and stayed with a pen friend and er … then she came and stayed with me in England, but I haven't worked with foreign people … no.

INTERVIEWER.Fine … er … have you got a full driving licence?

ANNIE.Yes, I have.

INTERVIEWER And er … can you drive a minibus?

ANNIE Yes, I drove a minibus when I was working with the youth club.

INTERVIEWER Fine, that'd be very useful. Er … the job is initially for six months … how would you feel about staying beyond that if we asked you?

ANNIE.I'd be happy to stay on … very happy to stay on longer … if it was possible, yeah.

INTERVIEWER And what have you been doing up to now? I mean what was your most recent job?

ANNIE Erm … well, my most recent job … I was an assistant to a vet, actually, for the last six months.

INTERVIEWER Interesting … why did you decide to leave that?

ANNIE Well … I wasn't trained for it … I was doing it on a part time basis and … really I was looking for a job more involved with people.

INTERVIEWER Well, why do you think you'll be good at this job?

ANNIE Er … well, er, I like being around a lot of people, I like the kind of life where there are a lot of activities going on you know, films, parties etcetera.

INTERVIEWER Yeah, yeah OK,well thanks very much. Perhaps you … if you'd like to visit the college now and I'll see you again after lunch.

ANNIE OK, thank you.

INTERVIEWER Right, thanks very much for coming.

UNIT 4

LESSON 10 ACTIVITY 2

INTERVIEWER Melanie, what makes an ideal holiday for you?

MELANIE Well, it has to be somewhere reason … reasonably cheap as I'm not earning a lot at the moment, erm, I'd like warm weather to be

guaranteed … erm … I like to be active, erm so somewhere with lots of sports facil … facilities so I can go sort of water skiing, swimming and that sort of thing erm, because I hate sort of lying on a beach all day … erm … and I don't like sightseeing … I find that very boring. Erm … in the evenings I'd like to go to lots of different sort of local restaurants – so somewhere with er … sort of interesting foods and local drinks and and all that sort of thing.

Erm, last year I did a round the world trip which lasted nine months … erm … I managed to get a really cheap air ticket. Erm … I went with two girl friends from university, er which is very important, because it's really important to share sort of all the experiences with them … erm I wouldn't have liked to have gone on my own I don't think. Then, I might now, I don't know. Erm … we went to India, Thailand, Australia, New Zealand, Hawaii, er … Canada and California and then back to the UK. Erm … I learned a lot about lots of different cultures and met lots of people … erm … I think I became very independent and quite a sort of strong character and everything … erm … and it also sort of got travel out of my system … and was a sort of bit of a final fling before settling down and starting a job … erm … it was very good fun. Erm, I enjoyed Thailand a lot … erm … mainly because it was the country that's most different from our culture. We were there for six weeks and it was a very erm, easy country to travel around erm, in the sense that the people were very friendly, and we felt very safe there. Erm we had sort of the bright lights and excitement of Bangkok and then we spent a couple of weeks on this gorgeous sort of paradise island called Ko Samui down in the South and we also went trekking, erm, up with the hill tribes for a week, which was an absolutely amazing expreience..

Erm, I also enjoyed Australia a lot because we actually sort of got more settled there. We were there for five months, and we erm, we worked and lived in Melbourne for six weeks and rented a flat and earned money by waitressing and erm, selling over the telephone. We … we got lots of jobs like that because of our English accents. We even all took on pseudo names … I think I was Olivia Flight and Jack was Abigail Arden White and things like that – but it was really funny and we did earn quite a lot of money and it was good fun.

LESSON 12 ACTIVITY 3

TRAVEL AGENT Hello. Breakaway Tours, can I help you?

MRS WALLIS Oh yes, good morning. Erm, my name is Mrs Wallis and recently you booked me into the Flatford Country Club in the Lake District for a couple of nights.

TRAVEL AGENT Oh yes, I remember Mrs Wallis. How are you?

MRS WALLIS Oh, I'm very well. Well it … it was moderately successful… erm, but to begin with you do say in your brochure that a minibus meets trains at the station.

TRAVEL AGENT Yes.

MRS WALLIS Well, when I arrived at five forty five there was no minibus, sadly.

TRAVEL AGENT Oh … oh I'm sorry about that … er, that. Er did you ever find out why?

MRS WALLIS Oh no, I'm afraid I didn't. Erm … er I was forunate though, I got a lift, but it could've been extremely awkward.

TRAVEL AGENT Yes, of course.

MRS WALLIS And erm secondly, I w … I was very disappointed because I'd taken my little dog with me it's wonderful walking country, but alas, they don't allow dogs in the club and so he had to spend all the time in the local kennels, and I think really you should put that in your brochure … er, that dogs aren't allowed.

TRAVEL AGENT Er … yes, I see … er, well, I'm … I'm … I'm sorry. Erm, you see, er … in fact it's a … it's a fairly new club we're dealing with. We've only been with them for about three months and er, nobody else has mentioned that before. But er well, yes we will have to try and do something about that.

MRS WALLIS Oh good. Erm … this is just a minor point really, but you do mention in the brochure tennis courts in … in th … in the plural. But in … in fact there's only one, so it … it does get rather booked up and er… sadly I was unable to get a game which, really was quite irritating.

TRAVEL AGENT Ah, yes, well … there … there are in fact quite … just one moment … but there are several squash courts, aren't there?

MRS WALLIS Oh yes there … there are indeed, excellent … but I'm afraid I don't play squash and I had taken my tennis racket and … and was rather disappointed

TRAVEL AGENT Yes, I do see.

MRS WALLIS Yes erm … well you see I … I would have complained to the owners themselves because I think you said it's … it's a hospitable family concern which sounded so nice, but erm I'm afraid they were away … well, I mean it was early February, so they were probably on holiday … that's fair enough … but … but you see this is why I'm … I'm telling you so that you can put these points in your brochure. Oh, erm, I'm afraid also there were no guides to be found locally… .

TRAVEL AGENT Er, right … yes … oh dear, you … erm … you seem to have had rather a bad stay er, really don't you. Erm I mean the rooms are very nice, aren't they?

MRS WALLIS Oh … oh yes. Yes. It's … it's a very very nice place. It's … it's beautifully done and … and …there are lots of nice things to do and … and it is good walking country. It's … it … I just thought I'd mention these points … I mean, I think that if you put them in your brochure – about the dog and … and everything, you know, it … it would be very helpful.

TRAVEL AGENT Er … OK, well … thank you very much Mrs Wallis … erm … we'll try and get on to that and see if we can make some changes and, thank you very much for calling and telling us

MRS WALLIS Oh, it's a pleasure.

TRAVEL AGENT Bye bye.

MRS WALLIS Bye bye for now.

UNIT 5

LESSON 14 ACTIVITY 4

First Speaker

I like ballet, classical ballet and modern ballet and I like like both dancing myself and watching ballet in the theatre … and I like listening to music, classical and also sometimes to pop music, but I prefer classical. Er … and I like going to parties, private parties, but sometimes I need relaxing at home … be by myself. Erm … I do not very much like going out to bars which are very crowded and have very loud music. Erm … and erm … when I meet people at first, I don't think I seem very open erm … and I can never make decisions as I'm very easily influenced by what people tell me … and I'm not very hard … I'm easily hurt.

Second Speaker

I was born in Stratford on Avon, which is erm … of course, the home of Shakespeare, but er, for the last few years I've been living in Norwich. Erm … as for my interests, I'm very interested in cinema, but I also enjoy travel and photography. Er … I'm a novelist … I've published one novel, but er … when I'm not writing I like to do a bit of English teaching. I suppose I would describe my personality as … as having two sides. On the one hand, I'm quite outward–going, but for various different reasons I've become more reserved than I was when I was younger. Erm, I'm … I like to think of myself as quite generous and sensitive.

Third Speaker

I live in Bristol, I've only lived there for a … erm couple of months. Before that I lived in Spain erm … bef … and I've lived in lots of other different places. I lived in … in Barcelona for two years, and I've lived in London and all over the place. Erm … I like listening to music. I like all sorts of music: classical music, jazz, rock, and I play the drums. I play the guitar and I sing sometimes. Erm … I would describe myself as a thoughtful person. I think I'm reasonably intelligent … erm … and people tell me that I'm sensitive. I would like to think that I'm artistic … er … however, I think sometimes I'm a little bit selfish.

Fourth Speaker

I enjoy play the piano; above all, classical music. And I like going to the disco and meeting foreign people. And I don't like sport … er … except swimming. Friends say I talk a lot, and I think that I'm very happy. And I'm studying to be a civil engineer.

LESSON 15 ACTIVITY 2

MRS DUVALIER OK then, le … let's have a look

SIMON Which hand?

MRS DUVALIER Your right one. Oh, that is quite interesting. I think you are someone who is interested in ideas – you enjoy reading … that right? And discussing things er … with your friends. Erm … you're a very rational person – perhaps too much – and I suspect you are impatient with people, people who are too emotional about things … is that right?

SIMON Erm well … yes, I … I suppose that is true … yes.

MRS DUVALIER … and I think sometimes you take things too seriously. You should er … you should learn to relax more. This part here … just there … well that shows you're very much a man of the er … of the mind. I mean, you're … you're generous and kind, I mean, people admire you and things like that … and I think you make friends easily … people like you … is that right?

SIMON Well, well … I don't know … I … I hope so … I'm not really sure.

MRS DUVALIER … I'm sure they do … well, I can tell you they do. Now then, what about your family life? Oh, quite strong, I think … this line here, though.

SIMON Yes …

MRS DUVALIER … it shows a very strong attachment to your mother.

SIMON Oh.

MRS DUVALIER Your mother rather than your father.

SIMON Oh, really …

MRS DUVALIER Yes. Are you not aware of this?

SIMON No

MRS DUVALIER Well … any rate, that's … that's true, that … that line there … that shows that. Your family, you see, it's very important to you. Now le … let's have a look at the other hand.

SIMON Sorry … one moment …

MRS DUVALIER Er … That's right. This'll tell me about the future. Oh … oh … I can see a lot of travel. Yes, there … this is the traveling line, here. Erm … let me just have a look at the other hand as well. Er … yes. It's this one here, you see, this … this hump here. This shows you're going to spend a lot of time overseas.

SIMON Oh really?

MRS DUVALIER Yes, but I don't think you'll be very satisfied with your time overseas …

SIMON Oh dear

MRS DUVALIER No. I think you'll be a bit unhappy while you're there … but when you come back …

SIMON I will come back?

MRS DUVALIER Oh, you will definitely come back … and when you come back everything will be much steadier, you'll be on firmer ground when your back here, you see …

SIMON I understand.

MRS DUVALIER Yes. And this is when you'll meet your wife.

SIMON Oh.

MRS DUVALIER Yes. You won't meet her abroad, you'll meet her here … when you are about, erm … thirty–two, and it'll be a happy … happy life … very happy life. And let's see, let's see … children … erm … yes, that's one … two … three children

SIMON As many as that?

MRS DUVALIER Three, yes definitely three. Er … two boys … oh no, wrong about that er … it's two girls and a boy. This line, it gets a bit confused, that's why I wasn't too sure.

SIMON Oh yes … but … but … de … but definitely three … three children.

MRS DUVALIER Yeah three … three children … definitely three. And er … erm … er, you'll have good health.

SIMON Oh.

MRS DUVALIER Oh yes, you will.

SIMON Oh, that's reassuring.

MRS DUVALIER You'll live to a … a good age. You'll see your children grow up, you will. Er … this line here, that suggests you'll live right into your eighties.

SIMON Oh.

MRS DUVALIER Oh, maybe even into your nineties. Let's have a look at your other hand. Er …yes, oh that confirms it … very long life …

SIMON Oh, well, I … I'm relieved, good.

MRS DUVALIER Quite a lot of money too. I don't think you are going to earn it yourself, though. I … I think you're going to inherit it, or … you might win it . Do you gamble?

SIMON No … not much.

MRS DUVALIER Oh well … No, then … then you'll inherit it, I think. So, that's quite satisfactory, don't you think?

SIMON Well, yes … er, fairly comprehensive, thanks very much, That was … er … very, very interesting. Thank you.

MRS DUVALIER Right.

UNIT 6

LESSON 17 ACTIVITY 4

INTERVIEWER Now Ky, I'd like to ask you about your trip from Vietnam to England. Can you tell me when you left the country?

KY I left Vietnam on 27th September 1978.

INTERVIEWER And why did you leave?

KY I left because we were … I … we were trying to escape from a war and my parents didn't want me to join the military service in the country

INTERVIEWER Fine. And … erm … how did you leave the country?

KY I left Vietnam by boat … erm … it was a fishing boat about fifty foot long and … erm … there were a hundred and sixty two people on the boat so it was slightly crowded.

INTERVIEWER And what … what did you have eat and drink?

KY Erm … we had mainly fruits and er, biscuits really, because it was the fir … it was the first time for most people on that boat and we were all very seasick due to the weather conditions, mainly.

INTERVIEWER How … how long did the sea-sickness last?

KY That lasted about two or three days for most people, after that we all got used to it.

INTERVIEWER Did you know where you were going?

KY No … erm … as far as I was told the helmsman was aiming for somewhere towards Malaysia across the South China sea … erm … he told us that we had enough fuel and food to go across that stretch of water … erm … but any further I don't think we wo … we would have managed.

INTERVIEWER And how long did the trip take?

KY The trip took about a week … er… well, we actually met the Malaysian navy after seven days … it was … we were actually near Malaysia at the time and, erm … they took us to a refugee camp, which was actually an island.

INTERVIEWER Erm … what were the conditions like on the refugee camp?

KY Erm … terrible, to say the least … erm … there was no fresh water and what water we could find by digging wells soon got contaminated and er … there was no food at all, there was no fruits growing on the island and er … the United Nations had to bring in rations for the people living on there.

INTERVIEWE Di … did you live in, er … huts or on the beach or, or what?

KY Well, we had to live on … in huts … erm … and we had to build the … those ourselves by chopping down trees on the island and the trees on the island soon got used up as well, despite there were plentiful of it.

INTERVIEWER And … so how did you spend the time there?

KY Erm… sometimes … I spent most afternoons on the beach swimming … erm sometimes we'd go gathering wood erm… and sometimes we had to carry the water… the fresh water that's brought in by tankers from the beach to where we lived – so they were the main occupations on the island really.

INTERVIEWER And when … when did you leave the island?

KY I left in July 1979 to come to Britain.

INTERVIEWER After how long was that?

KY That's ten months of being on the island.

LESSON 18 ACTIVITY 5

INTERVIEWER Ted, how are you going to cope with life on a desert island?

TED I'll take it as it comes, I think … er, Sue.

INTERVIEWER You're good at looking after yourself, I mean, you can cook and …

TED Er … I can cook and er … I have a fairly leisurely out look and I take things as they come.

INTERVIEWER What … you're going to build yourself a shelter or … or what … what will you do?

TED Er, yeah … a few palm leaves and … kip down under that.

INTERVIEWER Oh, it sounds lovely, it so … now you're allowed to take a cassette., What would you have? What would you choose?

TED Er …that's … that's easy, er … sixties was my formative time and, er … it would have to be the Beatles. Abbey Road.

INTERVIEWER Lovely. And you're allowed to take a book. What's that going to be?

TED Erm … I'm quite a science fiction freak, you know, Bradbury and Asimov and so on … so, erm … the simplest thing would be a collection of any science fiction stories

INTERVIEWER Right, just any science fiction. And of course, you ma … can have er … a useful object. Now, what would be useful on this desert island?

TED Well, erm … I couldn't have a full set of tools, presumably, could I?

INTERVIEWER No, no, no, no.

TED No way? Erm, well the next best thing … erm … one of those Swiss Army knives with everything on it, you know.

INTERVIEWER Well that's almost as good really, isn't it?

TED Almost.

INTERVIEWER Great. And you're allowed a luxury item.

TED Well er … a luxury item … I mean it's like a part of me, really, but I couldn't go anywhere without my guitar, 'cause I plan to write a whole new collection of songs and er … by the time I come off the island I shall be armed with a … a whole new batch of work.

INTERVIEWER Happy memories of this – so it sounds rather luxurious – desert island you're going to have. And you're allowed an animal. Now, what's the animal you'd choose?

TEDS Well, with my luck er … this desert island probably wouldn't have any animals on it … and I always …

INTEREVIEWER No, I don't think it has … you … you can choose an animal to take with you.

TED … I always imagine desert islands with monkeys … so, could I take a monkey?

INTERVIEWER You can certainly take a monkey with you

TED Thank you very much.

INTERVIEWER Thank you very much Ted.

TED Thank you.

UNIT 7

LESSON 19 ACTIVITY 3

LODGER Well, … it's erm … it's a very nice room. I wonder if the …

LANDLOR Good, I'm … I'm glad you like it.

LODGER Yes, yes, erm … Perhaps we could just go through one or two points.

LANDLORD Mm, certainly.

LODGER erm … just to clarify a few things. Erm … about the bathroom … erm … would it be possible to have a bath every day?

LANDLORD Yes, that's… that's … that's no problem … yes.

LODGER Erm … and, erm … are there any special times when you'd like me to use it?

LANDLORD Well, we… we normally say once a day, but er … at no particular time during the day. That's er … that's up to you.

LODGER I see, so erm … is there hot water all day?

LANDLORD Yes, yes … yes there is.

LODGER I see … right. And … erm … about cooking, erm … is it possible to … to use the kitchen at any time to cook?

LANDLORD Erm … yes, but erm … you must remember that my wife and I also use the kitchen and so we say normally that erm … other people should er, use the kitchen before eight o'clock in the morning and after half past seven in the evening.

LODGER Right … erm … would I be able to have friends to the house?

LANDLORD Yes … erm, but erm … not overnight. Er … we would not be too happy with that, I'm afraid.

LODGER Erm … if I did want someone to stay overnight, just occasionally, erm … might it be possible to find an arrangement?

LANDLORD Well, no, we have no accommodation in … in the house, but perhaps you could find accommodation in a guest house nearby or a … a hotel … erm … I'm not sure, maybe you ought to talk to my wife about that.

LODGER Right, OK. And erm … do you allow parties?

LANDLORD Yes, erm … maybe not quite … too often but … erm … as long as they're finished by twe … twelve o'clock midnight … erm … and also, of course, we would like you to tell us about any party you intend to … to have.

LODGER Mm … I see. Erm … would I have access to the telephone?

LANDLORD Yes er … the system we have normally is that erm … everyone puts the money for the calls they make in a little black box which we keep on erm … the table next to the telephone … erm … and there's one other point – incoming calls – we think it's … it's … reasonable that there should be no incoming calls after eleven o'clock, simply because we we … we think that that could disturb other people in the house.

LODGER Right, yes. Do you … do you allow smoking in the house?

LANDLORD Well, I'm afraid I have to say no. We have discussed the matter and er … no one else in the house smokes, so I'm afraid we have to say no.

LODGER Yes, right, I see. And erm … and would I have a key to the front door and a key to … to the room as well?

LANDLORD Yes, we give … er … excuse me, we give

everyone a ... a key to their room and to the front door of the house and er, well, naturally we say please don't lose it and do not give it to anyone else.

LODGER Right ... OK ... well, I ... I think that's about it as far as I'm concerned.

LANDLORD Erm ... well, there's another couple of things er ... I'd like to mention before you do make up your mind. We do say also that there ... there is er, no music or television in the house after half past eleven ... and another thing ... could you bring your own towels ... but ... er, sheets and blankets are, in fact, provided.

LODGER Oh great! So I ... I wouldn't have to bring my own sheets?

LANDLORD That's right, that's right.

LODGER Ah, I see right ... thanks very much. Right, well thanks. Erm it ... it's a very nice room and erm ... and I ... I think I'd like to take it if that's alright.

LANDLORD , fine ... that's fine.

LESSON 20 ACTIVITY 2

ESTATE AGENT Mr Ellis...

MR ELLIS Yes.

ESTATE AGENT Come in, come in ...

MR ELLIS Good morning.

ESTATE AGENT Well, here it is ... let me erm ... if I may, point our a few of the features before we start our little tour. As you can see, it's in a quiet, residential area. Er, there's a good school close by and er ... you probably saw there are some shops just around the corner.

MR ELLIS We passed the shops, yes.

ESTATE AGENT Right. Well, the house itself it's er ... it's Victorian. Er, there's a large garden ... er ... which we'll see in a minute. Er ... it's erm ... terraced. Er, the walls are very thick, so there's no noise from neighbours, so that's all right er ... you can ... you can make noise too and they won't hear you.

MR ELLIS And erm ... and it's centrally heated I see.

ESTATE AGENT Yes. Yes, it's centrally heated throughout.

MR ELLIS Good.

ESTATE AGENT So, shall we er ... shall we have a little look around?

MR ELLIS I'll ... I'll follow you.

ESTATE AGENT Oh ... all right. So this is the hall, obviously.

MR ELLIS Yes ... quite small, aren't they, these Victorian ...

ESTATE AGENT Yes, yes ... yes they are ...they ...they were all like that as you ... every house along here is like that. If we turn left here, this is the sitting room.

MR ELLIS Ah, yes.

ESTATE AGENT Yes. It's er ... it's quite large, as you can see.

MR ELLIS Lovely room, yes.

ESTATE AGENT Now there's an attractive open fire ... er ... don't know, do you like an open fire?

MR ELLIS Yes indeed, yes.

ESTATE AGENT Good, good.

MR ELLIS And that overlooks the ... er ... the road.

ESTATE AGENT Yes. Yes. And er, it's got everything else ... er ... power points and so on.

MR ELLIS Yes, fine. I've seen that, I think.

ESTATE AGENT OK. Er ... into the next room then

... there we are ...

MR ELLIS Out into the hall?

ESTATE AGENT Out into the hall again, and left again. Now this room has been used as a study ... want to use it as a study.

MR ELLIS I can see that ... it's got shelves and ...

ESTATE AGENT It's got shelves and er ... yes. Oh and there are some double doors here. Now these double doors ...

MR ELLIS A view over the garden.

ESTATE AGENT Well it leads to a patio ... a paved patio ...

MR ELLIS Yes, oh I see.

ESTATE AGENT ... which leads down into the garden.

MR ELLIS And that would be south facing would it?

ESTATE AGENT South facing.

MR ELLIS So we could eat out ther in the summer

ESTATE AGENT Oh yes. And there's a very attractive lawn and flowerbeds, fruit trees ...

MR ELLIS Fruit trees ...

ESTATE AGENT Yes. And there is of course a door from the patio which ... er takes you into the kitchen.

MR ELLIS Directly into the kitchen.

ESTATE AGENT Yes. Erm ... well shall we have a look at the kitchen.

MR ELLIS A look at the kitchen ...

ESTATE AGENT ... from the inside.

MR ELLIS ... back into the hall.

ESTATE AGENT If we come back into the hall and turn left here. This is the kitchen.

MR ELLIS I see.

ESTATE AGENT It's large and er ... a lot of natural light ... of course fully fitted.

MR ELLIS All these cupboards ... all these cupboards new?

ESTATE AGENT Oh yes it's fully fitted, fully fitted

MR ELLIS Very good indeed. Lovely. Thank you.

ESTATE AGENT Right? Out into the hall again. And, here we are, up the stairs to the first floor. Now, the first room at the top of the stairs here ... er ... is ... is the er ... the first bedroom. That's about the same size as the kitchen.

MR ELLIS And this overlooks the garden as well.

ESTATE AGENT Yes, it does, yes.

MR ELLIS Oh, that's a good view, isn't it. It's lovely

ESTATE AGENT Yes, it's nice, isn't it? And the built in wardrobes you can see there.

MR ELLIS I see. Yes. Good.

ESTATE AGENT All right? Out again and along

MR ELLIS Erm ... there'd be another bedroom ...

ESTATE AGENT Yes, just along here ... on the right hand side there's the second bedroom.

MR ELLIS Well, considerably smaller ...

ESTATE AGENT Well, slightly smaller. It's still a generous size, of course.

MR ELLIS Yes ... yes. This could be the boys' room, I think.

ESTATE AGENT Oh really? Yes. It could be, it could be. Erm ... OK?

MR ELLIS Yes, that's fine. And what would be this room next door?

ESTATE AGENT That's ... er ... that's the bathroom. Good sized bathroom as you can see.

MR ELLIS Oh yes. And a shower ...

ESTATE AGENT Oh yes ... yes.

MR ELLIS Very good.

ESTATE AGENT And finally just er ... just here, down here to the right ... out of the bathroom ... this is the ... this is the spare room.

MR ELLIS Aha. Guest room, probably.

ESTATE AGENT Well ... or you could use is as a store room.

MR ELLIS Indeed, indeed. And that's it, is it?

ESTATE AGENT And that's it.

MR ELLIS Thank you very much.

ESTATE AGENT Pleasure.

LESSON 21 ACTIVITY 3

INTERVIEWER So, how long have you been living here?

MRS PEDLEY Er ... we moved in 1971. We're getting used to it now.

INTERVIEWER It's a very big er ... house. How ... how many rooms are there?

MRS PEDLEY Erm ... we have eight bedrooms and six bathrooms. I'm not sure how many rooms downstairs, but they're all large so it looks probably as though it has much more than it has.

INTERVIEWER And how much land have you got around the house?

MRS PEDLEY Er ... sixty–six acres ... twelve acres of garden and eight acres of water, parts of the moat ... still, you see.

INTERVIEWER You must need er ... a lot of people to help you look after it.

MRS PEDLEY No ... no, er we have one gardener ... erm, that's it.

INTERVIEWER You do all the rest yourself?

MRS PEDLEY Yes, yes ... and we have been without gardeners, which was preferable to having bad gardeners. Er ... but at the moment we've just for six weeks had a gardner who we hope is going to be good. Erm this is going to make a lot of difference to us.

INTERVIEWER Now, I understand you were a teacher before?

MRS PEDLEY Erm ... I taught children between five and seven mostly. My husband was also a teacher. Erm ... but he hated it. He taught woodwork and maths and he couldn't stand to see the children spoiling lovely pieces of wood. It made him ill and the doctor said get out before it kills you and so he did.

INTERVIEWER Right ... so now you live in this beautiful old house. Erm ... do you miss teaching?

MRS PEDLEY Erm ... no, I'm much too busy to miss it. Neither of us miss it. He was pleased to be out of it, because we now have a furniture factory which is reasonably prosperous ... allows us to live here any rate, which is very expensive.

INTERVIEWER Are there any disadvantages of being rich?

MRS PEDLEY Erm ... no ... not that I can think of. Er we don't ever think that we're rich. We have sufficient money ... not too much ... to do more of less what we want to, but my husband still says that we shouldn't travel first class on an aeroplane, we should go economy, which upsets me enormously. He says, you know, those extra thousands of pounds could come in useful for building a wall, which is true. Erm ... so we ... we don't think we're rich.

INTERVIEWER So would you like to earn more money?

MRS PEDLEY Erm … probably, yes …

INTERVIEWER How would you spend more money?

MRS PEDLEY I don't think we would need to spend more, actually. We're quite happy with what we've got. Erm … we do also have our own aeroplane which is a seven–seater twin, so this enables us to catch up in our leisure time … what would take most people two or three days to do we can do in a day. We can always be back home again at night which is what we like. We can have lunch in Paris, lunch in Amsterdam, go to the Isle of Man, Jersey all in a day and back again … erm … so on a Sunday we can have the whole weekend in a day.

INTERVIEWER And you travel first class in your own aeroplane?

MRS PEDLEY Of course.

UNIT 8

LESSON 23 ACTIVITY 2

INTERVIEWER Mike Trees, you do a lot of training with experienced athletes, but what advice would you give to people who are taking up running for the first time?

MIKE It's very difficult to give general advice for people who are taking up running because of the different standards of fitness. For example, a man who's been sitting behind a desk all his life and has done very little exercise would only be able to do maybe a hundred metres jogging and a hundred metres walking and maybe continue that for about ten minutes. That sounds very little, but if he's been sitting behind a desk it's very hard work … whereas a young boy or a young girl who are fresh from school and have been doing lots of sport may be able to run for twenty or thirty minutes without a rest. The important thing is the speed. You run at the speed that you feel comfortable at, and for fitness the most you really need to do is about thirty minutes three times a week. Any more than that and you'll get into serious running where you improve for racing.

INTERVIEWER Now, for people taking up the sport … do they need any special clothes or shoes?

MIKE Well when you're getting started you need to consider the shoes. The shoes are very important. In some ways you pay for what you get. If you buy a very cheap pair of shoes, they won't be very good for running and you'll probably get injured very quickly. However, don't get the top name in shoes because with the most expensive shoes you're purely paying for the name … somewhere in the middle I would say. It might cost you about £30. It sounds a lot of money, but to get a good pair of shoes and to ask the advice of a salesman who knows what he is talking about is very important. The clothes, though, are very unimportant. So long as you're warm, you can run in anything at all, so in that respect running is quite cheap.

INTERVIEWER Finally Mike, do you have any more advice for beginners

MIKE Well before you start to run, it's very important to warm up correctly. This means doing some stretching, loosening up the muscles, because if the muscles are tight you'll pull them, and it will cause a lot of problems later on.

The only other thing to add is before you go running: don't eat for about two hours. Again, it sounds a long time, but it's very very

uncomfortable and very difficult to run on a full stomach of food.

And finally, if you follow this advice you'll hopefully become addicted to the sport like I have. I can think of nothing better than running on my own through the countryside in the middle of summer, away from everything, part of nature. It's very relaxing.

UNIT 9

LESSON 25 ACTIVITY 3

INTERVIEWER Richard, how many snakes have you got at the moment?

RICHARD Erm … I have three at the moment … erm … a Boa Constrictor, which is probably the best known snake … erm … a python … erm … and a little corn snake … erm … a sort of rattlesnake of the same species, … erm … just a little baby.

INTERVIEWER Have they got names?

RICHARD Erm …yes, they have actually. Erm the little python erm … is called Kirstie … erm … the big Boa Sparkie and the little rattelsnake is Toad.

INTERVIEWER Toad?

RICHARD 'cause it bites me. It's called Toad

INTERVIEWER Now, what do you have to do to look after a snake?

RICHARD Erm … basically erm … keep it warm … erm ple … provide it with plenty of water, erm … it must never dehydrate, although they look … many snakes are desert living, so it's quite surprising really, but erm … they do need to keep them with water erm … and a constant supply of food. Erm … not too big an enclosure otherwise erm … they get lost almost … erm … which is quite surprising, since the enviroment they live in is normally very vast, but erm … most snakes prefer to be kept in a smaller container. They feel more secure.

INTERVIEWER Now, what do they eat?

RICHARD Erm … rats, mice, erm … small rodents… things, that sort of thing … normally, like, once a week or twice a week, you know, not much more than that.

INTERVIEWER Where do you get the rats from?

RICHARD Erm … well, I get them from a friend actually, but erm … you do get specialized pet shops that'll help you out and sort them out for you and don't mind killing them … which isn't pariculary nice to watch or anything, but erm … has to be done, really.

INTERVIEWER Now, are any of these snakes dangerous?

RICHARD Erm … the big one is very strong … erm … all snakes must be classified as quite dangerous really erm … because of their such sharp teeth and quite enormous strength for their size, but erm … not dangerous as such, unless you're being silly, you know … erm … that sort of thing.

INTERVIEWER Have you ever been bitten by one of your snakes?

RICHARD I have … erm, it's not too painful, though … erm, it makes you jump more than anything, because it's so quick, erm … well staple action really …

INTERVIEWER Now, not many people keep snakes … why … why do you like to keep snakes?

RICHARD Erm … good question … erm …I don't really know, actually … erm … I think they're beautiful creatures, erm … many don't … erm …

fascinating to watch, erm … very strong, agile creatures, erm … superb movers erm …

INTERVIEWER What does your family think about it?

RICHARD Erm … they're not too bad actually. Mum … Mum and Dad like snakes. Erm … my little sister does … doesn't mind them at all now, although if she'd grown up without them … then I think she, like many, erm …she'd be told that snakes aren't nice things. Erm … Dad's a bit dubious to the bigger snakes … erm … Mum's not too bad at all.

INTERVIEWER Have you ever had any accidents in the house? I mean … has a … a snake ever escaped?

RICHARD Yes, it has actually … erm … sometimes if the phone rings and you're in the middle of cleaning them out erm … and you leave the glass door open or something, and you come back and think 'oh dear' and you've lost a snake, erm … but normally it's OK … erm … they don't normally go far. You have to be a bit careful they don't go under the floorboards.

INTERVIEWER So you've never lost one?

RICHARD No, I've never actually lost a snake.

INTERVIEWER How expensive are they to buy?

RICHARD Erm … the actual snakes are quite expensive erm … as things … as pets go … averaging on er … mi … an average size snake I'd say you'd be talking about … erm … £50 to £80 … erm, but the rest of the set up is not too expensive. Erm, a cage might cost £25 erm … then the little bits and pieces and food isn't really much at all – so it's not too expensive once you're set up, it's just getting set up which will probably prove to be the most expensive.

LESSON 25 ACTIVITY 4

PRESENTER Our first caller on line three is Mrs Rushton from Coventry. Welcome to the show Mrs Rushton … what's your question?

MRS RUSHTON Er, thank you. Hello. Well, erm … I really want to know what you have to do when someone suffers from exposure to cold. Er you see, erm … I often go mountain climbing. And it really is my greatest fear, this … being stranded overnight in very cold conditions … or actually finding someone who's suffering from this condition and … and I'd like to know, you know, how to handle it please.

DR BRADLEY Yes. Well now, er Mrs Rushton … erm … the person should of course er be kept warm and any wet clothing removed and … and then the person must be dried, of course. Erm … they must be covered with blankets, if possible, and given erm … warm food and drink. It's important to remember that no alcohol should be given. That can be serious. And a doctor should be consulted as soon as possible.

PRESENTER Thank you Dr Bradley for that advice. Now I'd like to turn to our second caller on line two who comes from Bournemouth. Mr Rose, what's your question?

MR ROSE Er … I'd like to ask the doctor please, erm … what to do when someone is bitten by a poisonous snake.

DR BRADLY Yes, well, there's only one er … poisonous snake in Britain, Mr Rose. Er, the procedure would be different of course … from … from this if you were abroad. But most important is that the person should be kept relaxed. And er

... the area of the bite must be washed in water. Er ... and the part of the body that has been bitten should be supported and kept off the ground. The wound should'nt be cut, and ... seek medical help for young children.

LESSON 26 ACTIVITY 2

DR LAWTON I'm often asked if individuals can do anything to protect the environment. People say to me 'Isn't it something for governments to do?' On the contrary, there are many ways in which we as individuals can help and it's essential that we act now, before it's too late. In fact, in some cases it's already too late and the quality of our life is seriously threatened.

Firstly, and most importantly, I think, we can save energy. And there are many ways we can do this. For example, if you're going on a short journey, don't take the car, take your bike. Turn off the lights in your house when you're not using them. And when you're cooking, it's wasteful to have your cooker, whether it's electric of gas, at maximum. Turn it down to the minimum temperature. And lastly, most houses in Britain are grossly overheated... now it's possible to reduce the temperature of your house by anything up to five degrees and still be perfectly comfortable.

Now secondly, normal petrol, which you use in your car, gives off lead into the air. And recently the government has been trying to promote lead-free petrol, And this is indeed much better for the environment ... happily it's becoming more and more available from garages and it's cheaper too. It's actually 10p a gallon cheaper, so you can encourage your friends and relatives and people you work with to use lead-free petrol.

Thirdly, many things can be recycled ... means they can be used again. And number of local authorities have bottle banks where you can take your used wine bottles and they can be recycled. Something else that can be recycled is paper. There are now paper depots that you can take your waste paper to – newspapers, computer print-outs ... all sorts of things, paper of all types ... and that paper can be then reused.

Again, the ozone layer is being destroyed by a number of things, one of which is aerosol sprays. Recently supermarkets and department stores have begun to sell enviromentally friendly, ozone friendly, aerosols – and really I do advise that these should be used wherever possible.

Furthermore, you can use organic food. It's possible to buy food from stores which has not been treated with pesticides and fertilizers. They are more expensive yes, but they're much better for you ... and, of course, they're better for the environment as well.

Well lastly, and I think this is a very important step, you can join a local action group like Greenpeace or Friends of the Earth, and you'll get leaflets and information on ways in which you can help save the environment and encourage other people to do the same. They need your support, so I urge you to join one of these societies as soon as possible.

LESSON 27 ACTIVITY 5

REPORTER How many different animals have you got here in this zoo?

KIM Well, we've got about 200 different species altogether.

REPORTER And how did you get the idea to start this zoo?

KIM It was started by my father, really. He used to keep a pet shop in London, but he got fed up with that and decided he wanted to start a zoo. It was almost like a hobby at first, but then it grew and now the whole family work here.

REPORTER I see. Some people say that zoos are cruel places. What do you say to that?

KIM Well, this is now a very old fashioned idea. In fact, I prefer to call this a wildlife breeding centre rather than a zoo, because our main aim here is to preserve and propagate animals – especially those which one day may be threatened with extinction. The animals here all have enclosures according to their needs; so some animals have tall enclosures, because they need to climb, while others have long enclosures, because they need to run. I get annoyed with those who think that enclosures are like prisons; they don't understand what we are trying to do here. Zoos used to be exclusively entertainment centres, but Linton is a centre for the preservation of species which has become necessary because of the thoughtlessness and greed of the human race. There are so many animals which are at the present threatened with extinction such as the ... the panda, the tiger, the rhinoceros, for example.

REPORTER So the main aim of the zoo is to preserve species?

KIM Yes, that's right. But we also hope to educate the public by giving them more information about the animals. Some animals have been badly represented in the popular imagination – I'm thinking of the typical horror films, for example, where spiders, sharks, bats, snakes, etcetera, are always seen to be terrifing creatures which attack or threaten humans, whereas in reality they don't.

REPORTER These animals don't attack humans?

KIM No, they only attack when their lives are threatened by humans. Secondly, we want to educate people to appreciate their environment and learn what needs to be done to protect it. Some people still buy animal furs of threatened species or jewellery made of ivory from elephant tusks or ashtrays made from gorilla's feet. So long as people can do this, we still have work to do.

REPORTER Which of these animals have you bred successfully here?

KIM Oh, nearly all of them have bred except those which are too young to breed. Our biggest triumph of recent years was the Toko Toucan, as we were the first zoo to achieve this. The Toko Toucan comes from Brazil and is rather difficult to breed from as it's a very clumsy bird and manages to break its eggs quite often. Our pair called Pablo and Benita broke all three of their first clutch of eggs, and we were lucky to rescue one egg from their second clutch which we eventually hatched in an incubator. They are also rather expensive to, keep as they must be kept at a warm temperature, so we have to to keep them in a heated enclosure with special bushes and plants; and then they like fresh fruit and vegetables which they eat vast quantities of.

REPORTER What problems do you have in keeping this zoo?

KIM Well it is expensive to run. We have to feed all the animals, obviously, and then provide enclosures for them all. For example, our enclosure for the Sumatran tiger cost £30,000. Then we have to pay our staff. We have to pay for electricity, for facitities which the public expect, for the occasional vet bills, and so on. Two years ago we had to spend a lot of money for repairs to buildings caused by floods and a hurricane.

REPORTER Well, thank you for talking to us and we wish you luck with the zoo in the future.

UNIT 10

LESSON 28 ACTIVITY 3

EMMA Well, of course, you must remember that when I was young, we didn't have all the luxuries that you have now. We lived in a very small house in Devon ... very small but ... but cosy. I lived with my mother and my two sisters. I was the oldest and ... and my father was usually away, because he was in the navy, and of course was often travelling around the world, so I had to help my mother look after the house and my two sisters.

INTERVIEWER Wha ... what was the house like?

EMMA Well, as I say, small, but we were happy there. There was just a kitchen and sitting room downstairs and then two bedrooms and ... and a tiny room with just enough space for one bed ... that's where I used to sleep.

INTERVIEWER What about a bathroom?

EMMA Oh no, no bathroom ... no bathroom. When we wanted a bath, we had to heat up the water and then have a bath in a wooden tub in front of the fire. We only had a bath about once a week and ... on Sundays, usually in the evenings ... and the toilet, the toilet was outside in the garden, so if you wanted to go in the middle of the night you had to put on a coat and slippers.

INTERVIEWER What about heating?

EMMA Oh yes, we had heating ... well, not central heating like nowadays, but we had what we call in Devon a Bodley ... a Bodley, yes, which was like a big stove where we burned wood and coal ... oh that was in the kitchen, but it used to heat the whole house and ... and we cooked on the top of it. And, of course, ... we ... we didn't have fridges in those days, so we stored all our food in a ... in a larder. You couldn't keep food like you can now ... you can go the supermarket and do all the shopping for the whole week if you want. Then we used to go shopping nearly every day and my my ... mother oh, she enjoyed it, you see ... she liked to meet the people in the village and get all the gossip.

INTERVIEWER Well, how did you spend your time?

EMMA Well, we didn't have television, of course, and for a large part of my youth we didn't have the radio either. We played a lot of games I remember, and we ... we ... we read quite a lot, and I remember during the First World War we was always knitting ... knitting jerseys for the troops, for the soldiers who were fighting in France. We all had to do that. Er, now what else? Oh, well we actually lived by the sea, so we played all day on the beach ... building houses and castles with sand. We had quite an outdoor life really, and I'm sure we had hot summers then ... oh yeah I can remember the sun shining all day. Not like now when it seems to rain all the time ... we were quite poor you see, but oh, we were happy.